OVERCOME OVERTHINKING AND ANXIETY IN YOUR RELATIONSHIP

A Practical Guide to Improve Communication, Solve Conflicts and Build a Healthy Marriage

By Robert J. Charles, Ph.D., D.Min

Copyright © 2022 by Robert J. Charles - All rights reserved.

The content contained within this book may not be reproduced, duplicated or transmitted without direct written permission from the author or the publisher.

Under no circumstances will any blame or legal responsibility be held against the publisher, or author, for any damages, reparation, or monetary loss due to the information contained within this book. Either directly or indirectly. You are responsible for your own choices, actions, and results.

Legal Notice:

This book is copyright protected. This book is only for personal use. You cannot amend, distribute, sell, use, quote, or paraphrase any part, or the content within this book, without the consent of the author or publisher.

Disclaimer Notice:

Please note the information contained within this document is for educational and entertainment purposes only. All effort has been executed to present accurate, up-to-date, and reliable, complete information. No warranties of any kind are declared or implied. Readers acknowledge that the author is not engaging in the rendering of legal, financial, medical, or professional advice. The content within this book has been derived from various sources. Please consult a licensed professional before attempting any techniques outlined in this book.

By reading this document, the reader agrees that under no circumstances is the author responsible for any losses, direct or indirect, which are incurred as a result of the use of the information contained within this document, including, but not limited to, — errors, omissions, or inaccuracies.

Table of Contents

Your Free Gift 1

Introduction 3

PART 1: Becoming Aware of Your Overthinking Issues 7
    Chapter 1: Overthinking: A Sword in Relationships 9
    Chapter 2: Overthinking vs. Healthy Communication 29

PART 2: Attending to the Problem 47
    Chapter 3: Steps to Overcome Overthinking and Anxiety Issues in Your Relationship 48
    Chapter 4: Solving Conflicts Quickly: A Hack 65
    Chapter 5: How to Prioritize Healthy Communication over Overthinking 85
    Chapter 6: Dealing with Negative Energy, Thoughts, and Habits in Your Marriage 105

PART 3: Preventing Relapses and Keeping Things Going 118
    Chapter 7: The Art of Listening, Trusting, and Loving Fiercely Listening: More Than Just Hearing 119
    Chapter 8: Preventing Overthinking Relapses to Prevent Conflict and Trust Issues 144

Conclusion 163

Thank You 167

Bonus 168

References 172

Your Free Gift

As a way of saying thanks for your getting this book, I'm offering the

book *Enough Overthinking* for FREE to my readers.

To get instant access just go to:

https://go.robertjcharles.com/EnoughOverthinking

Inside this book, you will discover:
- The physical effects of overthinking in your life
- How overthinking can destroy your mental health
- How ruminating and worries will damage your social life
- And so much more

If you want to finally be free from overthinking for good, make sure to grab the free book.

https://go.robertjcharles.com/EnoughOverthinking

You will also receive a Free Bonus

Download Your FREE 30 BIBLICAL PROMISES TO OVERCOME ANY CHALLENGE

Click: https://go.robertjcharles.com/30BiblicalPromises

At some point, everyone on this Earth faces a tough challenge. Help is on the way! God has your back. His Word will empower you to face any trial or tribulation.

These 30 promises from God will give you the strength and resilience you need to move forward. To get your FREE 30 BIBLICAL PROMISES TO OVERCOME ANY CHALLENGE.

Click on this link:

https://go.robertjcharles.com/30BiblicalPromises

Introduction

Marriage is never going out of style. It will never become old news. I know, I know, that's a pretty bold declaration, but I can be sure of this because humans are social animals, and we can never deny one of our most crucial needs: the need for companionship.

Intimate relationships are great, but nothing brings a man and woman as close as marriage. Yes, marriage comes with many benefits; however, it also involves many responsibilities. It's sort of like owning a private jet. There are a whole lot of perks that come with it, but if you look beyond the cushioned seats and open bar, you'll see that you've got to keep that baby running, and that is only possible when you're able to take responsibility.

Communication is the oil that marriage relies on to function. Without effective communication in a marriage, the moving parts of the relationship begin to experience wear and tear. Over time, there'll be so much rust that the whole thing will fail altogether. Overthinking, which is the main focus of this book, is the enemy of effective communication in a marriage. If you're an overthinker and you've been worried sick about how this habit is affecting your relationship with your significant other, you're in the right place. This is where you're going to deal with it once and for all. I won't sugar-coat facts in this book, because I believe you're here for the truth.

Overthinking and anxiety are a problem for so many people. I've seen them ruin relationships–romantic and platonic alike. What happens is almost like something out of a book or movie: someone thinks something is real when it isn't. They spend time believing the lie and working themselves up until they're soaked in a big, murky bowl of unreal thoughts. Their thoughts then affect their perception and their behavior. Things begin to get out of hand if the thoughts go unchecked.

Divorce is ramping up in our society. Many new marriages will end in divorce. I wrote this book to help you not be part of these statistics.

When you go into a relationship, you lay down a part of yourself in the inevitable exchange of vulnerability. Because you expect the other person to trust you and have faith in you, you must do the same. Anyone who has come to this point in a relationship expects to be treated well, and it only makes sense if they flinch when things don't seem to be going as planned.

You're permitted to flinch. But you should not permit yourself to overthink. Especially as a habit.

When you've found the one you love and care about, the least you can do is honor them and focus on real thoughts instead of mirages. Wondering if they're happy with you? Ask. Ask instead of imagining they're not. Ask instead of overthinking whether they honestly need some alone time or they just don't want to talk to you.

I just punched you with the power of communication over imagination. I've got more punching where that came from. The goal is simple: to equip you with these truths that'll help you to overcome this nasty habit that's ruining your relationship.

Maybe you're looking out for yourself too much.

Looking out for yourself isn't bad, and I can't say you should feel guilty for doing that. But when does it become too much for comfort? Simple. When you begin to get paranoid doing it. It's very easy for an overthinker to become paranoid because the thoughts just go from one level of negativity to another in a spiral of doom and gloom. I get that becoming vulnerable comes with some fear of being betrayed, but your fear can make overthinking worse and ultimately cause a breakdown in the relationship you cherish.

You've got this.

By and large, I'm very sure that you're going to be fine. Yes, it will take some work, a mental shift or two, redefining a couple of things, and some healthy actions to back it all up. It'll take work and determination, but I'm sure you've got those, and I'll be really glad to walk you through this journey. I will also be presenting to you a biblical perspective on some aspects of overthinking, especially as it pertains to your relationship with your spouse. I hope you'll enjoy the read and the journey. Get ready for an eye-opening ride.

PART 1

Becoming Aware of Your Overthinking Issues

The other day, I watched my dog sit on her mat in the corner and chew on a bone I got for her. Every time I turned my head to look at her, she'd stop chewing, lick her lips, and sniff in my direction as if trying to detect a silent command. She'd wait for as long as I held her gaze, blink rapidly, and if I still said nothing, she'd whine a bit. Eventually, she'd pick up her bone and continue chewing, but a few seconds later she'd turn to look at me again and find me still staring at her. Rinse and repeat.

I always chuckled to myself after each episode of this. But more than finding amusement in my dog's behavior, I was bewildered by her level of awareness.

—**Grace**

Awareness is a powerful concept. Oftentimes, humans seem to have trouble being aware. It's almost as if someone else has to point out to us what we're doing right or wrong (especially wrong!) before we even realize that we're doing it.

The first part of this book deals with awareness because that's the first step to solving any issue. You need awareness that you have a problem, as well as an understanding of the nature of that problem. This is what opens the door to the possibility of a solution.

So, let's become aware of what overthinking is exactly. Let's see how overthinking might be affecting our relationship with our spouse. Let's go gain some perspective.

While you're going through this book, I want to ask you for one small favor. Could you please consider writing a review on the platform? Posting a review is the best and easiest way to spread the word about this book and support healthy relationships in the lives of so many couples.

CHAPTER 1

OVERTHINKING: A SWORD IN RELATIONSHIPS

"Overthinking, also best known as creating problems that are never there."

–David Sikhosana

Whose mind goes on tours when they're alone at any time of the day? Yours. Whose mind takes the express train through lands, seas, and mountains? Yours. If you've identified yourself in both of these scenarios—sweet! You definitely qualify for this ride.

We've all been there at some point, trapped in the overthinking spiral; some are still in it (no shame there). Downslopes in relationships are at the heart of many hurts that we go through as individuals. But what's at the heart of those downslopes? Suspiciousness? Insecurities?

It's human to have thoughts. It's expected and even healthy. You aren't a robot. You need thoughts to make your day-to-day decisions. And it's normal to act on your thoughts. The thought of a certain special someone may pop up now and then in your mind like a phone notification, except this notification is not bothersome or a thorn in the flesh of your focus; you revel in how sweet and special this person is to you. You daydream about the present and about the beautiful future of togetherness that awaits you…

…until the missiles of "what-ifs" and "maybes" attack your blissful ride. Thinking is good. Imagining is good. Yes, even getting lost in your thoughts is okay from time to time. The dicey part involves one thing and one thing only: the content and quality of your thinking.

What's overthinking all about?

Everyone who has a soul is able to think. In fact, thinking is crucial to being humane and rational. But—and here's the big but—there are times your thinking oversteps its bounds. One minute you thought your partner was the best person in the world; the next minute, you think she or he is a villain of some sort. Soon, you both are trying to fix broken parts of your relationship because of some thought that popped into your mind. Pretty miserable, isn't it?

Have you ever caught yourself creating some *masterpiece* of anxious thoughts in your mind that revolves solely around a change in the tone of a person's voice, their attitude, or the words they use? Like, involving no real facts, just your perception of the situation. Well, have you? Sure you have! I mean, why else would you be reading this book? Bingo.

For example, you might wonder why someone's voice seems lower than normal, leading you to think about why he or she didn't add your name to a morning greeting like other times... Yikes! What torment! You then begin to read between the lines, investigating things that should have been allowed to just die a quick, natural death. But no. You dwell far too long on your suspicions and assumptions, get moody and cranky, and start seeing unreal realities.

Patterns like these are all too common with people who are letting overthinking ruin their relationships. With time, a feeling of resentment that you never intended to have begins to build up inside you towards your loved one, and accusations eventually set in. Depending on how far your mind has traveled on that non-issue, overthinking has the capability to ruin things for you completely. You'd be shocked.

When you start to sense that your thoughts are beginning to spiral out of control and you're obsessing over little things, whether they were done or not done, said or not said, it's indeed time to rein in your brain.

Understandably, overthinking can be born out of past experiences. Maybe you were ghosted by someone in the past, and it was only later you began to realize all the signs that were playing out right before your eyes. That might have contributed to your becoming someone who finds it difficult to take anyone at face value. In other words, it's hard to ever trust again. It might be that you often replay conversations in your head, then beat yourself up every second for not giving the perfect retort to that bully at work. Yeah, the list seems endless.

It would be unfair to ignore the fact that past experiences can mold your identity and perspective. Past experiences can affect your interactions with others. It gets really bad if you're a victim of abuse. I empathize with you, I really do. It's not your fault that your views about life and certain groups of people have been distorted by an experience that left your heart and mind scarred. Trust me, I know it's frustrating when you can't help but see the worst in a situation or person, even when that person has good intentions. If you see how your overthinking can affect your relationship, leaving you with more hurt, you can take that huge step towards changing the pattern of your thoughts.

How Overthinking and Anxiety Affect Your Relationship

Overthinking and anxiety can have devastating effects on relationships that start out with so much promise. Overanalyzing can wreck mental health and leave you and your partner hurt. Your partner will feel grossly distrusted when you see everything wrong in every single little thing they do or say– or don't say.

Real quick, let's move straight to the non-negotiable things that happen to your relationship when you overthink. You probably already know these, but it makes sense to list them out here at this point, just in case you actually don't know how rapidly overthinking can make your relationship into a huge mess.

1. Lost trust

No one enjoys being mounted with heaps of accusations. Your pessimism and paranoia will definitely wreck the heck out of your communication level. When communication is lost, loopholes are created for mistrust to grow. Simple.

2. Mental exhaustion

Your significant other is liable to become exhausted when they have to explain and re-explain everything to you. They will, no doubt, become exasperated about the conclusions and assumptions that you come up with perpetually. This is the point where they begin to avoid having conversations with you or even avoid you completely. No one enjoys being subjected to constant interrogation about whatever accusations your mind has concocted. And if you continue doing this, you'll end up feeling exhausted yourself.

3. Constant conflict

Constant confrontations and overanalyzing make you come across as a cranky, unhappy person who's looking to pick a fight. If the other person isn't comfortable with your accusations, a counter-confrontation is bound to occur, leading to deeper conflict. Words that you never meant to say can be forced out of your mouth in that state of anger.

4. Inability to live in the moment

Your "what-ifs" and "maybes" are keeping you from creating beautiful memories with your spouse. You'll often end up ruining the present that promises to lead to a beautiful future. The moment you start second-guessing everything, you won't enjoy your relationship anymore. A relationship that's meant to make you happy can become the reason for constant bouts of anxiety, all thanks to your overactive mind.

5. Reliving past traumas

As a victim of trauma, it can be difficult to accept the beauty and goodness that's in front of you. It can seem too good to be true that your life is going well. Give overthinking free rein, and pretty soon it'll seem reasonable to start self-sabotaging. Your emotional well-being (and that of others) is affected when you replay your trauma in your head and use that old brush to paint those who want the best for you—especially if it's your spouse. As they say, "hurt people hurt people." Don't allow past trauma to become your current reality.

6. Frustration and constant fights

When you find yourself picking fights about the minutest of things, you have most likely become sad and anxious. At some point, you might even loathe your present self and begin to wonder how you got to that state. From self-loathing, depression sets in. Of course, the resulting breakdown in your relationship will leave you even more frustrated.

7. Health problems

Are you the type who never vents or lets out some steam? If all you do is keep mute and allow those poisonous thoughts to eat you up, guess what'll follow shortly thereafter? Yep, health issues. When anxiety sets in, the body often responds with increased heart rate, nausea, decreased immune function, low sex drive, chronic exhaustion, and so on. You can't enjoy your relationship if you aren't healthy yourself. Your body responds to what your mind tells it.

Clearly, overthinking does more harm than good. Scratch that! Overthinking does NO good. This is not to remind you of or make you feel regret about your past relationships that did not work out (possibly due to overthinking). This is just a step in the right direction–identifying the problem and the havoc it has caused and seeking a way out. That's exactly why you're reading this book.

Signs That You're Hyper-Analyzing Specific Parts of Your Relationship

Hyper-analyzing your relationship is one sure way to demolish all the bricks of trust and harmony you've built together. You use the poisonous "what-ifs," "maybes," "shouldas," and "wouldas" to dissect everything that might be wrong in your relationship. (You could win first place in a math competition if you considered applying that hyper-calculative part of your mind to a more useful pursuit, you know.) Here are some signs that you're hyper-analyzing your relationship:

You see "no" as a total rejection

This attitude screams "six-year-old who doesn't take no for an answer." You've probably seen or heard of a kid who cries and whines about not getting the answer they want. If you're acting like this (but the grownup version), you've got to change your mindset. Life won't always give you what you demand, and neither will the person you're married to.

Before you take offense, ask yourself, "Do I say yes to everyone, always? And when I say yes, do I sometimes wish I had said no?" There are times you say yes and realize it's to your own detriment, right? Now, where am I going with this?

1. A "no" could be because what you're asking is not convenient for your partner. Respect that and remember the times they've come through for you. Don't allow your selfishness to ruin your relationship simply because your partner is unable to agree to your needs at a certain point in time.

2. It could mean your request triggered your partner the wrong way, and they'd rather maintain whatever

boundaries they've set. If your partner feels uncomfortable, let it go.

A peaceful relationship is a bad sign for you

Were you raised in a toxic environment, ridden with conflict? You might have grown to believe that a relationship must be dramatic. This is a wrong perspective about love. Love doesn't have to be tough; it doesn't have to be nasty and dirty. It might come with challenges, but the goal is to recognize that the enemy is the challenge itself, not each other.

You apologize too much

Yes, there's such a thing as apologizing too much. Apologies happen because you did something wrong, right? If you're always making the wrong moves, you'll always have to apologize, and that can be a wake-up call to examine your thinking patterns since actions are controlled by thoughts.

Sometimes, however, it's not that you're actually doing all the wrong things; it's just that you think that you are. If you have a string of failed relationships, anxiety might develop at the beginning of a new one. You might then overthink your actions and feel you must be doing something wrong. This might a result of emotional abuse you experienced at some point in your life where someone degraded you verbally. They may have told you that you never do anything right, for example, making you jittery and full of apologies for things you shouldn't have to apologize for.

You're afraid your partner might leave you

Fear of abandonment and rejection become engraved in our heart right from childhood. If you begin to see every challenge in your relationship as a threat that they'll leave you, it might be a sign that you're overthinking certain aspects of your relationship.

You overthink every irregularity

Relationships and marriages sometimes hit the rocks because one partner reads a trivial situation wrong. If you're someone who believes that life runs on the principle of one-size-fits-all, you're in for a rude awakening. But that doesn't have to be a bad thing. Instead of assuming the worst, flip the thoughts to the positive: What if this is the perfect person for you? What if your partner isn't playing you like others have in the past? What if your spouse's silence doesn't mean they're holding a grudge?

Gaining Awareness of Your Overthinking

If you want to get out of your own head, you need to acknowledge that being stuck in there is a real problem you need to deal with. Recognize that you can be a stumbling block in the path of your happiness through your thoughts. Don't spray the garden of your life with diesel fuel when there's a freshwater stream nearby. Being aware of your thoughts by paying attention to them is a journey you must be willing to take.

Take a deep breath. Inhale slowly, then exhale slowly. Done? Now, stop thinking about the process of doing that breathing exercise. You're overthinking again. Take a deep breath. Great! See, that wasn't difficult. Here's how to gain awareness of your overthinking in general.

Pay attention to the trail of your thoughts

Being aware of how your thoughts begin and end can be a great reawakening for you. If you notice that you're replaying events or conversations between you and your partner, that's dangerous ground. You might end up exaggerating unimportant situations or building resentments that weren't there initially because you have a habit of rehashing events, replaying the day, and reconsidering every single word your partner said.

A soldier needs to know the wiles of an enemy before making a move. Right now, get into "studying yourself" mode. See yourself as a fighter who's bent on winning a battle. Your mind informs most of the decisions that control your life. Now, it's time to fight.

Do you have negative thoughts when you're stressed out? Do you find yourself feeling unworthy when you scroll through feeds on Instagram or nice pictures of your friends having fun on their WhatsApp stories? At what time of the day do negative thoughts come to you? Does loneliness contribute to the back-and-forth your mind takes? These are ways to study and analyze how your thoughts come together in order to fight them.

Acknowledge that you're exaggerating

Recognize that your "what-ifs" are preventing you from being kind to yourself. Instead of thinking about the worst-case scenario, acknowledge that you just might be feeding your mind with too many negatives. Overthinking is like bringing a bull into a china shop; it's taking too much potential damage and ruining the things that are more important to you. Are you thinking you might lose your husband if you don't scroll through his phone? Or that your wife must no longer love you because she's not answering your text? These are negative thoughts that can make your spouse feel suffocated and untrusted if they find out what you think of them. Love should be liberating, not suffocating.

Take action to solve the problem

If there's a problem, the most reasonable thing to do is to fix it. The central purpose of this book is to show you how to go about fixing the problem. When you keep fixating on the bad thing that happened, you won't solve anything. You might even end up compounding the struggle with your overactive mind. Instead of constantly ruminating over the way your spouse responded to you at breakfast, have you considered talking to them about how it made you feel? Have you considered telling them how you'd like to be spoken to? Have you discussed with your partner your triggers? Do they know your boundaries? You'll save yourself a lot of headaches if you can be open to fixing a misunderstanding instead of rehashing it in your head.

Practically Speaking

Now that you're beginning to realize why and how your thoughts keep hovering like an uncontrollable drone, you need to schedule moments for private reflection.

Reflections are the opposite of rehashing. With reflections, you'll begin to see things more objectively. You'll see that other people aren't necessarily the problem, but you. Unlike rumination, which can lead you into a dark hole of self-sabotage, when you reflect, your eyes are opened to how you can handle matters differently.

You can set a timeframe (say 30 minutes) for worrying, ruminating, and rehashing. Allow yourself to mourn and grieve over the plans that didn't go well. Once that period is over, dust yourself off and get into something more productive. The moment you discover that overthinking is taking up time you could be using for other important things, be quick to remind yourself that you'll revisit that distressing thought later, during your next rehashing session. This method can help you get started by keeping your mind from constantly wandering.

The popular saying that an idle mind is the devil's workshop isn't far from the truth. This saying makes me imagine a creature with horns, holding a pitchfork and standing behind someone who just wants to sit and brood. Whichever way you choose to see it, when you create a vacuum, an empty space in your mind, something must occupy it. If you're engaged in projects that are worthwhile or hobbies that hold promise, negative thoughts will have no space to perch. You'll feel more relaxed and energized to take on whatever comes your way. So, get busy! We're not talking about merely distracting yourself, mind you—it's about *living*. Start living.

Let's Back Up a Bit

Is overthinking all bad? Hmm. Actually, the answer a straightforward yes, but the problem lies in folks confusing overthinking with critical thinking. They're two different things.

An analytical mind is, I daresay, an intelligent one. I once had the privilege of watching my friend interview candidates for hire in his outsourcing company. He wanted to hire an HR professional, and he had "brainy" as one of the qualifications for the ideal candidate. I chuckled when I saw his notes on this. Without flinching, he said, "Only a brainy one can hire brainy ones." But of course! When I dug further, he explained that what he was really looking for was a person with a highly analytical mind. "That sort of person," he said, "will be able to understand whatever problem we have and is the exact kind of person to look out for to fill the role."

Well, true. Having an analytical mind helps you do the high-level thinking involved in reviewing a problem and finding the solution. Analytical thinking is, as the name implies, done for analysis with a view toward finding a positive outcome. Overthinking, on the other hand, is thinking without a purpose or direction. It's thinking in scattered ways that open doors for stress and anxiety. Overthinking is just thinking and thinking, making mountains out of molehills and still arriving nowhere—basically, going around in circles.

Reasons Why You're Overthinking

I won't indulge you by helping you lie to yourself. You weren't born an overthinker. As a child, you took more risks, you were daring, and you thought you could conquer anything. Once you set your mind to achieving something, you went all-out for it. Little wonder you had no cares in the world. You thought the best of everything; you held no record of wrongs done to you by your friends; you laughed more and loved more. Great times, huh?

You see, something changed you. Let's take a look at how you got here, and the reasons why you might be overthinking.

- You were hurt by someone who betrayed your trust.
- You were abused as a child, leading to insecurities and doubts.
- You were constantly put down by people who should have lifted you up, leading to low self-esteem.

- You're a perfectionist.
- You love to attract sympathy from others.
- You're procrastinating and avoiding responsibilities.
- You overgeneralize and create stereotypes.
- You're afraid of conflict.
- You don't dare to live with uncertainty.
- You don't feel comfortable not being in control.

Do these descriptions sound like you? A couple of them, right? Life changes us in the most unexpected ways, and unfortunately, sometimes that means we have to live with some negative consequences. But there's hope.

Stress, Anxiety, and Overthinking: The Terrible Triplets

Your everyday life is bound to come with stressors, whether it's a fight with your spouse, a job that drains the heck out of you, raising a troubled kid, or so many other factors that come with living in this world. You can get stressed when your body, feelings, and thoughts respond to these external events. Dr. Melanie Greenberg, a clinical psychologist who wrote *The Stress-Proof Brain*, defines stress as "a reaction to environmental changes or forces that exceed individual resources." From this definition, there are circumstances beyond our control that might leave us disturbed and helpless, leading us down a toxic thought-rollercoaster. You might feel drained and your stress levels might increase.

Some symptoms that you experience while you're under stress include rapid heart rate and shallow breathing. When it gets chronic, the body becomes overactive in this state of stress, potentially leading to life-threatening outcomes like heart disease, high blood pressure, or a breakdown of the immune system.

Stress encourages anxiety. Other effects of stress on your mood are restlessness, lack of motivation and focus, feeling overwhelmed, irritability and sudden outbursts, insomnia, depression, and, of course, overthinking.

How does overthinking come into the picture, exactly? According to Amy Maclin, when something unfortunate or stressful happens, we tend to immediately think back to other times they felt horrible or stressful, leading to a pileup of toxic thoughts—a factor that "sets the stage" for an overthinker to keep roaming until she or he reaches a slippery slope.

Like stress, anxiety is also a response to a threat—but it's a response to a threat that does not exist, a story you've created in your head, an idea that's not real. For example, say you're asked to present a business proposal at a board meeting. You've prepared all the slides that you need, yet your heart is pounding so fast, and you wish it would stop; your palms are sweaty and you feel hot even in an air-conditioned room. These are symptoms of anxiety.

Guess who the threat is here? Nobody but the voice in your head. You've created a narrative in your head that's making you think that you might flop. You're thinking they might not like it.

You've concluded that your proposal is crap. You're beginning to mourn its rejection before the actual presentation. This narrative that has been created as a result of your overthinking has triggered fear (anxiety) in you.

When anxiety steps in, it interferes with your sleep, relationships, productivity, and other aspects of life. Stress and anxiety are intertwined with overthinking. When there are issues beyond your control, you tend to stress over them and overthink them, leading to chronic worry and anxiety. Both anxiety and stress cause overthinking and are amplified by overthinking. These damaging triplets are interwoven. To break the cycle, you have to discover what informs your thoughts. Could they be coming from a place of stress or anxiety?

Wrapping Up

The bottom line is that overthinking isn't in any way healthy for your relationship. The sad fact is that it tends to go along with a lot of other unsavory habits, like stonewalling. Have you heard of stonewalling? If you haven't, don't worry; we'll talk about it in the next chapter. I'm pretty sure it's something you might have done before, or perhaps you do it often.

In the next chapter, we'll take a look at the difference healthy communication makes in a partnership compared to overthinking. You might not be aware of how damaging your habit is to your relationship, and that's what I'm about to show you.

Your Quick Workbook

What reasons have you identified for your overthinking?

_____
_____
_____
_____
_____
_____

In what two instances has overthinking ruined a nice day, outing, or relationship of yours?

_____
_____
_____
_____
_____
_____

Do you have a past trauma that you haven't dealt with which might be making you overthink?

_____
_____

_____

_____

_____

_____

Which would you regard as the main fuel for your overthinking: stress or anxiety? Why?

_____

_____

_____

_____

_____

_____

CHAPTER 2

OVERTHINKING VS. HEALTHY COMMUNICATION

"Most misunderstandings in the world could be avoided if people would simply take the time to ask, 'What else could this mean?'"

—Shannon L. Alder

I remember one night when I was exhausted from work, I lay down on my bed to catch my breath as my mind wandered to my boyfriend of three years. He was the one person I needed to rant to about my day. Since he wasn't picking up his phone, I scrolled through my WhatsApp to see if he was possibly online.

"He's probably getting tired of my calls," I thought as I rolled my eyes. I turned this thought over in my mind, even when I knew he always picked up and returned my calls the moment he saw them.

"I'm sure he's online." My mind came up with another conclusion. And what do you know—I was right! I got irritated. So chatting with his friends on WhatsApp was more important than picking up my calls? I shot him a message and expected a near-instant reply. I didn't get one. I was fuming.

I flung my phone on my bed, stood up, and started pacing, still fuming. The clock was ticking, and he still hadn't replied. I returned to his DM. He was still online! I highlighted the text I'd sent to him and deleted it. Of course, WhatsApp helped me shout it from the rooftops that I'd deleted a message. I wanted him to see that I knew he was ignoring me. After 10 minutes that felt like 10 years, the customized ringtone I had set solely for him buzzed into the silence of my small room. Even though I was happy to hear from him, I wouldn't let the voice in my head go. I accused him of ignoring me.

We ended up in a heated argument following my rants. After I calmed down, my boyfriend explained he'd been on a family group call, so he could neither pick up my calls nor respond to my message. That misunderstanding separated us for a while.

I stressed myself and my boyfriend out for nothing that evening. I was in too much of a hurry to accuse him of something that had not been confirmed. I was not polite in my approach to him. I allowed my emotions to get the better of me. If I'd waited to listen to his explanation, I wouldn't have found myself in that mess of a conflict.

—Leah

While we mentioned earlier that overthinking harms communication, this is not something that should be addressed just in passing. Communication is germane to the smooth running of any form of relationship, be it platonic or romantic.

The older you get, the more you realize how much you need someone to be in your corner, to be there for you in the good times and the bad. You always want to be able to converse with the people you love and care about. They're the ones you call when something happens to you, no matter how irrelevant or minute it might seem. Since they love you, it's not a bother to them. When there's a communication breakdown, however, unresolved conflicts fester. This not only ruins your relationships, but it also clogs the wheels of your peace of mind. I've yet to find someone who rejoices when they're no longer in touch with a lover they cared about, especially when the terms of separation weren't healthy.

But where does this breakdown begin? Most likely in that moment you begin to imagine the worst possible scenarios, when you speak your mind in the most unacceptable ways, when words you never meant come spewing out of your mouth. Later, you may wish you'd been quick to listen and slow to speak, but by then the damage is done. Your relationship will become a theater of constant conflict when you continue to let the issues you create in your head to fester and flourish. It's high time you killed them off.

Stonewalling: The Abuse That Ruins Communication

I sat in my office once and received a couple. The man had eyebags and was dressed in a rumpled t-shirt with baggy jeans. He looked like he badly needed a shave. His wife had her hair done in a ponytail but didn't look anywhere near as put-together as she could have. They literally dragged themselves into my office and sank into the chairs. My first instinct was that they were having marriage problems because of some mismanaged grief. Perhaps they'd lost a kid, I thought. I stood to welcome them, but what I heard nearly knocked me off balance.

"I want a divorce!" the man said.

For a moment, I debated with myself whether to point out to him that I wasn't a divorce lawyer or to just sit down and let him speak. I sat down and chose to ask him why.

"She's an expert at stonewalling. She deserves a medal!"

The woman looked hurt but didn't say anything in her defense. It was a welcome change because I usually have to calm yelling spouses during sessions.

—**Benjamin**

Stonewalling is simply the act of ending a conversation abruptly or refusing to discuss something that needs to be discussed. Think about the silent treatment and completely ignoring your partner. Think about avoidance of an argument and total dismissal of your partner's concerns. Yeah, that's all stonewalling. It's not good. It's abusive. It eats marriages for breakfast. Don't do it.

If you find yourself constantly falling into the habit of stonewalling, you can learn to overcome it. The antidote is communicating. Rather than avoid or dismiss a conversation that should be had, choose to talk about it.

When you stonewall, you leave room for assumptions. You also leave many questions unanswered, and your partner ends up feeling unheard. Inflicting the silent treatment on your partner might make them think you're punishing or manipulating them. Are you punishing your partner? Are you trying to manipulate them? No? Then don't stonewall.

How to Communicate Properly If You're Overthinking

Let's imagine the story of Nina, a German monkey known for staying at the gate of her cage whenever tourists come by. For some weird reason, Nina never ate the bananas that were handed over to her. Whenever she was offered bananas by tourists, she always turned her face away in disdain.

One day, a young boy came by and, after getting the same reaction from Nina, decided to take her home. After offering her a lot of fruit and trying to get her to eat something, he gave up and left her alone for a while.

But fortunately for Nina, she stumbled across a piece of bread one day, and she ravaged it so much that the whole household was surprised! Apparently, it was bread Nina had wanted all along, but because she didn't (more specifically, couldn't) *say* so, she was never offered any and so had to starve.

The power of being able to communicate!

Communicating will save you a lot of pain in your relationship. You'll do yourself and your partner a lot of good if you communicate how you feel about something instead of jumping to conclusions or completely avoiding the discussion. When you learn to give your significant other the benefit of the doubt, conflicts are easily avoided. Try to gather facts rather than hovering around motives.

Communicating when you're dealing with overthinking is easier said than done. But if you and your partner have built a healthy foundation for your relationship, it'll be easy to discuss anything, including your overthinking problems. Whichever place you're at in your relationship or marriage, there's always a good place to start talking from. Let's look at a few useful tips to help you get started.

1. Be intentional

Healthy communication is something you have to make up your mind to do. Just like you can hardly get good grades by accident, it's impossible for your communication as a couple to "just work out." It won't. You have to be the one to make it work. You have to decide that you will do your part to keep the lines of communication open, even when you're tempted to stonewall.

2. Ask for a conversation politely

When you need to talk to your partner, asking for their attention nicely will help them to approach the conversation in a more relaxed manner. Instead of starting up abruptly or aggressively and risking them becoming defensive even before the conversation has started, it's smarter to ask nicely.

3. Discuss the problem when you're both relaxed

Discussions are best saved for a time when you're both relaxed. When blood pressure is running high, maybe you can politely ask for some time to mull things over and then return to the conversation when you're both calmer. This way, you'll actually get somewhere with your discussion.

4. Try writing it

A great way to communicate with your significant other is by writing to them. The blank page gives you a lot of room to express yourself, and it's neat because you can really express yourself there. Plus, it's therapeutic for you and your partner. This is where you give yourself the chance to say the things that might be difficult to express face to face, and you can go as deeply as you need to.

5. Prepare notes for a face-to-face talk

If you prefer the good old face-to-face kitchen table hash-it-out method, it can help to come with notes highlighting all the things you want to talk about. That way, you'll feel more confident when you do start the discussion and will be able to stay on track rather than get distracted by unnecessary tangents.

6. If you ask for their help, respect their feelings

Your partner isn't responsible for dealing with your overthinking, but they can help you by understanding and supporting your desire to work on it. When you're asking for their support, it's important that they know that they have a choice and that you'll respect their decision.

Examples of Conversation Starters to Overcome Stonewalling and Improve Communication

Trying to beat the tendency to stonewall your partner can be hard. The first few words are usually the most difficult, almost like you've got a piece of bone stuck in your throat. Having good conversation starters handy can help. You can try any of these:

1. It's really hard to talk right now, but we need to.
2. Can we talk?
3. Can we go for a walk together? You don't have to say anything.
4. I know you're angry, and that's okay.
5. Tell me why you're angry and I'll listen.
6. I'm sorry. (This is a good old classic conversation starter after a fight)

Some Conversation Starters That Don't Involve Talking

1. Leave a note in a conspicuous place for your partner to find. Here's a sample of what you could put in the note:

Hey, babe. I'm sorry our conversation ended in a fight. Gosh, we fight a lot these days, don't we? Are you up for a talk? Should we go out to that restaurant/park you love and grab something simple that we both love? I'm craving my favorite juice. What would you like?

OR

Hey babe. I feel so angry right now I don't know where to begin. I just want you to know that I have a few things I need to get off my chest. Please, can we talk?

2. Ask your partner to help you with something. Just ask. They might still be upset, but ask politely.
3. Buy them a tasty treat and write "peace offering" on a small piece of paper.
4. Send a text.

When trying to apologize or start a conversation with your partner after an argument, NEVER attempt to replace actual words or an apology or an in-depth discussion with a gift or even an act of kindness. If you buy them something they like or do something for them, it should be a means to an end: to defuse the tension and help the two of you start talking, not to erase the wrongs or make them go away. Ignoring the issues in your marriage is a mistake. Whatever issues you ignore are likely to come back to bite you…like a half-killed serpent.

Since this is such an important point, let me reiterate: Gifts and acts of kindness don't replace having an in-depth conversation about the problem or offering an apology for what you've done wrong.

Communicating with Your Partner is Key

Saying that communication is vital in a relationship is an understatement. Many relationships hit the rocks when one person stops talking for whatever reason. This means that keeping communication lines open is a matter of life and death for your relationship. You have to do it. If you're still passionate about making the relationship or marriage work, that is.

It's through communication that you'll come to understand each other's views on different issues. Your relationship will strengthen when you freely share your joys, hurts, opinions, fears, expectations, disappointments, and even boundaries. Think of the fulfillment and happiness that will spring up when you're able to freely converse with your partner on any topic. Of course, there will be moments of silence, but when good communication is a routine, that silence will never be awkward.

However, you need to know that not all forms of communication are effective. Effective communication requires putting yourself in the other person's shoes—in other words, having empathy. It's not just about exchanging words; it's about understanding the emotion and motives behind the thoughts you're trying to get across, and the thoughts your partner is communicating. Apart from this, you also need to listen to truly understand what's been said, which will make the other person feel heard and understood.

Why is effective communication important? Here goes!

1. It keeps your relationship fresh

Greg and Hannah were just about to be married when Hannah began to complain about no longer feeling a spark. Greg was so angry about this that he refused to work things out between them and left Hannah to go ahead with the breakup. It all happened so fast that none of their friends could comprehend what had happened.

Do you know what happened to them? I'll give you two guesses. Nope, nothing to do with disappearing butterflies. Yep, everything to do with communication. Somewhere along the line, they stopped sharing their hearts. They stopped talking. The result was inevitable.

Remember how your love journey started with that special someone and you always wanted to please them? You were always conscious of your attitude towards them. You would adjust the smallest strand of hair just to look perfect for them and take ages to decide on what to wear to a dinner date. Now that the mushy rollercoaster seems to have ceased and familiarity has set in, you need to get intentional.

You can't always depend on how you feel to do the right thing, you know. The desire to have things "feel right" explains why breakups and divorces happen: the end of the emotional tingling means an end to love for most people. But it doesn't have to be this way for you.

You don't have to be dependent on that emotional reaction that seems to lead you by the hand for every thought, word, and action. Take control and love hard. Be honest with your partner about your feelings. In doing this, it'll be easier to remember why you fell in love with each other in the first place. You're able to remind one another about what attracted you to each other.

If you keep talking, you'll always have stuff to talk about. The key: keep talking.

2. You'll understand each other better

It takes a lifetime to get to know a person. If people knew the implication and real meaning of "I want to get to know you," they wouldn't be in a rush to say it. You must understand that people evolve every second, every day, and every year, including you. Yep! You're not the same person you were yesterday. Understanding this will help you see the need to communicate your needs to your partner and ask questions. Constantly speaking about your needs will give you a comfortable space to know and understand not just yourself, but also that special person in your corner.

3. It helps clear things up

I remember feeling stupid after my boyfriend explained to me that the reason he couldn't pick up my calls was because he'd been in a group call with his family. I beat myself up that night for jumping to conclusions. If I had simply taken a chill pill and waited to hear him out or asked questions, we wouldn't have had a huge fight.

—Leah

When you allow little things like assumptions to become the truth you feed on, you ruin things. Here are three ways you can avoid making assumptions: ask questions, ask questions, and ask questions. Yeah, that's all. It's that simple. What happens as a result? You get an answer. Instead of overthinking whether the person could by lying, enjoy the moment and trust your partner. Your relationship will work out as long as you're with someone who is honest. Just breathe. Keep the lines of communication open always. Not once in a while—always!

4. It builds trust

When both parties are eager to communicate their thoughts and open up, there's room for vulnerability. One person doesn't feel left out of the other's life. You'll become one another's safe place—and isn't that the dream?

Leaving No Room for Assumptions

I expected my partner to always know how I felt. I wanted her to go all-out for me without me having to say a word. But my expectations were the root cause of most of the issues we were having. I disliked the fact that she wasn't aware of my feelings, and she absolutely hated the fact that I always pointed this out and made her feel bad about it.

—James

Unfortunately, mind-reading is not a gift we're born with. You'd think that in this world where effective communication is being phased out and couples are more often on their phones than in each other's arms, the ability to read minds would come in handy for us all, but sadly that's not an option.

In light of that, you simply must learn to talk to your partner to avoid assumptions. The following are what I call communication nuggets for overthinkers:

- **Your partner is not the enemy.**

One of the major reasons communication isn't effective is that we tend to take the offensive, leaving the other person with no choice but to be defensive.

It's a trap to think that you'll be able to get your point across by blaming or nagging your partner. Yes, your partner might have contributed in some way to your anxiety or stress, but at the end of the day, your priority should be making your relationship work, not playing blame games. In your communication, you must emphasize that whatever you're facing, you know you can get through it together.

- **Be completely honest and be prepared to hear what you don't want to hear.**

Okay, I know this is a tough one, but the truth is, your partner might not completely understand. Nobody understands overthinking as much as overthinkers. The most important thing is that you stay honest with each other, and make sure you're on the same page as far as your relationship is concerned and there are no secrets or hidden bitterness between you.

- **Focus on finding a solution TOGETHER.**

You shouldn't expect your partner to change overnight because of you. True, a relationship is about compromise, but it's also about understanding. What I want you to focus on is finding a balance that works for you both.

Let's say one of the triggers for your overthinking is your partner not replying to your texts right away. Try to consider their side first. You should be able to understand that it might not always be easy for them to instantly respond to your texts, and likewise, they should understand that this is very important to you and put in the extra effort. When having the conversation, try to find a balance. Don't be selfish and make demands that will be hard on your partner.

- **Tell your partner everything.**

Hiding things can make your communication futile. You've got to lay it all out without exception—your greatest fears, your past hurts, the things that make you anxious and second-guess the relationship, everything. Take your time, but know that it's worth the effort.

You can't lose with communication. Yes, being honest about your feelings is hard and painful, but if the relationship is important to you, know that there's no way it can thrive without you both talking about your struggles. Y'all signed up for summer, winter, and everything in between.

Wrapping Up

Now that we've identified the problem and we've talked about how communication is key, we still need to tackle overthinking as a whole. A lot of people who are overthinkers feel like they are doomed to be that way forever. They say things like, "That's just how I am. I can't change it."

What if I told you that it's possible to control that tendency to ruminate? Yep. It totally is, and that's what we'll be looking at in the next chapter. Let's jump in!

Your Quick Workbook

If your partner was the person overthinking, would you want them to communicate this problem to you, or would you prefer they kept it to themselves?

_____

_____

_____

_____

How difficult is it for you to communicate with your partner when you're overthinking?

_____

_____

_____

_____

_____

Why do you think it's hard to express yourself when you're overthinking?

_____

_____

_____

_____

_____

_____

Based on this chapter, what will communication help you with in your relationship?

_____

_____

_____

_____

_____

PART 2

Attending to the Problem

Have you ever thought about what it would be like if you didn't overthink so much? Have you tried to imagine how things would improve if that wasn't a problem anymore?

Maybe you and your spouse could actually work things out for once. Maybe you'd stop crying so much. Maybe you'd stop feeling like you need to break free from your head every day. Maybe you'd even be happier?

I invite you to take a moment or two to think about it. You know you have a problem with overthinking; you've seen the damage it causes. Think about how different things can actually be. This section will show you how to achieve this dream. The best part is that you can start applying these steps right away!

CHAPTER 3

STEPS TO OVERCOME OVERTHINKING AND ANXIETY ISSUES IN YOUR RELATIONSHIP

"To think too much is a disease."

—Fyodor Dostoyevsky

Your alarm clock wakes you up at 7 a.m. sharp. You roll over to turn it off and run a hand down your face. It took you forever to actually fall asleep because your mind wouldn't stop racing. As soon as you try to get out of bed, you remember that your partner didn't come to bed last night. Probably because of the argument you had two days ago. Now you wonder if they're avoiding you. Or if they don't love you anymore. Maybe you should get a divorce. But you know you still love them. But you can't trust them anymore. Or can you? Maybe you shouldn't have snooped through their phone and accused them of lying to you and falling in love with someone else. But…but then they should know by now the kind of person you are. Why would they be okay with getting that kind of message from someone of the opposite sex? They're probably cheating… Right?

You head downstairs for breakfast and discover that your partner already left. You sigh, tired of the awkwardness and stiff silences. You start to wonder if you should call, but then you decide they probably don't want to hear from you. You head to work and you're not able to focus much because you're thinking about your home situation.

A part of you wants to drop by their workplace to surprise them with lunch, but you know you'll see that person who sent them that text. You'd rather not disturb their idyllic workplace romance. Resentment starts to build as you think of all the other times your partner has acted in a suspicious way this past month—coming home late, not eating dinner at home, going to bed earlier than you.

The stressful thoughts in your mind take a toll on your work, and you find yourself snapping at your nice coworker. Great. Now she probably hates you too. You're relieved to leave work, and you head home again to fix dinner. You don't call your partner as you usually would on your way home. They probably don't want to hear from you.

You get home to find the dinner table already set up and your partner waiting for you with a smile on their face and open arms. You're surprised, but immediately your brain goes into overdrive: *Aha! I knew it! This is obviously an action fueled by guilt. They're obviously cheating on me. Why else would they do this?* You tell your partner you're too tired to eat at the table and take your food upstairs to eat in bed. You only manage to get two forkfuls down your throat before your thoughts make you restless and take away your appetite.

You start to imagine what life would be like as a divorcee. Everyone would whisper about how your spouse cheated on you because you weren't good enough. You'd have to find a new place to stay. You'd have to change your friend group. You'd obviously never go back to the same church again… Your thoughts whirl around your mind as you sink into a fitful sleep. You're probably going to wake up tired again tomorrow.

Hey!

Does this sound familiar? Overthinking can create so many problems where there were none to begin with, making your life bleak and joyless when it could be so much better.

Opening Up to Your Partner About Your Struggles with Overthinking

What's the best thing about being in a relationship? I've been privileged to talk to several people who are in happy relationships, and they unanimously agree that having a safe space to be themselves is the best thing for them.

I agree. Being in a trusting, healthy relationship gives you the space to be yourself to the fullest, without fear of judgment or desertion. However, being an overthinker can make it hard for you to communicate with your partner for so many reasons. For example, you might feel jealous of your spouse and doubt everything they say. You might have even considered following them whenever they go out or paying a surprise visit to their workplace just to make sure they're not lying. It's even possible that you've thought of hiring a private investigator to follow them just so you can breathe easy. Does that sound familiar? It's not unusual to overthink from time to time, but it could become a very serious problem if it's not taken care of quickly.

I think the worst thing about being an overthinker and having doubts about your partner or your relationship is loneliness. It can be pretty easy to feel isolated because you can't talk to anyone about what you're thinking. Most overthinkers try to deal with the intrusive thoughts by themselves, either by trying to ignore them or stifling them so that they don't sound irrational to other people. If you're in these very uncomfortable shoes, you need to do something about it. Having someone you can talk to anytime and share your deepest thoughts with will go a long way in helping you conquer overthinking.

You need to be able to speak to your partner and reclaim your safe space. You need to fight for the right to feel seen, loved, and understood in your relationship. You've gone without it long enough.

I can almost feel you rolling your eyes and thinking, "Wow, Captain Obvious much?" Stay with me here. Communicating with your partner as an overthinker goes beyond just saying whatever's on your mind at that time. Effective communication is something that sounds simple but can be very hard to achieve, especially when you keep trying and failing at it.

Before we talk more about opening up to your partner, you need to examine yourself and your relationship. Go back to what you wanted when you first started this beautiful journey you're on right now. Remind yourself of the love, promise, and excitement you felt when it all started. Remember how much your partner loves you. Recall that your partner is someone you trust. This means you can be sure that they always want the best for you and that they are reliable. Allow yourself to understand that your partner just wants to connect with you on the deepest level possible, and keeping them in the dark just robs them of that opportunity.

Another important thing to do before speaking to your significant other is to identify the source of your thoughts. What is at the root of your fear? For example, if you're worried that your husband is paying too much attention to his female coworker all of a sudden, it's possible that you're really just afraid your husband doesn't find you desirable anymore because of the weight you've put on. Identifying the source of your worries gives you and your partner enough ammunition to tackle your fears once and for all.

Now that we've laid the groundwork, here are some guidelines to help you communicate effectively with your significant other:

- **Have a face-to-face conversation.**

Conversations via text may cause confusion, as messages may be taken out of context and tone is difficult to decipher in writing. Keep in mind that you need to have an open and honest conversation with them.

- **Try to ignore your fear of rejection.**

This is the hardest step for some people. I understand that it's not easy to just ignore such a powerful fear, but giving yourself a mental timeout helps. Also, some techniques like meditation and distraction work here too.

- **Discuss your worries.**

Explain what you've been thinking and why. If you know the root cause of your fears, this would be a good time to discuss it. Ask your partner for space to talk and use statements that begin with "I." Avoid accusatory statements; instead, focus on your own feelings while reminding yourself that you value your relationship. Don't be afraid to ask for what you need, and remember to be as honest as possible.

- **Take regular timeouts.**

If the conversation gets off track or you can see signs that an argument is brewing, calmly ask for a timeout and pause. Evaluate the conversation to see how that could have happened. It's easy to fall back into old patterns of communication here, but taking as many timeouts as needed helps.

- **Be vulnerable.**

C. S. Lewis said, "To love at all is to be vulnerable," and I completely agree. Don't revert to defensive tactics to cover up emotions like anger, jealousy, shame, and anxiety. Instead, remind yourself that you are worthy of being loved. Loving yourself first helps you accept love from others. Involve your partner in your thought process as much as possible. Knowing that you have a companion to support you will help you feel less isolated and even improve your relationship.

Give yourself permission to receive the love and support your partner is bound to offer. If you're finding it hard to implement the guidelines above because your thoughts keep getting away from you, don't worry; the tactics we'll discuss in the next part will show you how to control your thoughts. Use these steps to guide you, especially when you're communicating with your partner.

How to Control Your Thoughts (A Step-by-Step Guide)

"Finally, brethren, whatsoever things are true, whatsoever things are honest, whatsoever things are just, whatsoever things are pure, whatsoever things are lovely, whatsoever things are of good report; if there be any virtue, and if there be any praise, think on these things."

Philippians 4:8

The ocean is really remarkable. It can be calm enough to let us frolic in its waters under the sun during summertime; it can also be cold and menacing, destroying entire countries and changing people's lives with a few tall waves. It can be docile enough to let us cruise all over it on its placid surface, and it can be powerful enough to submerge us without warning. But the danger doesn't mean people avoid the ocean or stop sailing. Instead, they've learned to control it, and many live successful lives on the sea.

Your thoughts are similar to the ocean: they can overwhelm and drown you, or you can choose to master them. Everyone should gain mastery over their thoughts, but for an overthinker, controlling your thoughts is an absolutely necessary life skill. When you control your thoughts, you can take charge of your life and position yourself for better outcomes all around. This step-by-step guide for doing just that is straightforward, practical, and it works. All you have to do is commit yourself to the process, remind yourself that you're deserving of love at every point, and watch yourself thrive.

1. Understand that thoughts are not reality

One mistake people make over and over again is believing everything they think. True freedom comes from the realization that our thoughts are just thoughts; they aren't reality unless we give them that power.

Thinking negative thoughts leads to having negative emotions, which leads to more negative thoughts and, in turn, negative emotions, and before you know it, you're stuck in a vicious cycle. These thoughts then become self-limiting beliefs, and you'll find yourself looking for evidence to back up those beliefs. Instead, distance yourself from your thoughts.

2. Observe your thoughts

Now that we've established that you're not your thoughts, you can observe them objectively. It might be difficult to categorize your thoughts when your mind is going at warp speed, but deliberately slowing down to observe helps. As you practice this often, you'll start to notice a pattern.

As you notice each thought, label it and let it pass. Labeling your thoughts will help you shed light on thought patterns and even handle your thoughts better. Using labels like "fear," "anxiety," and "jealousy" will help you understand how you're feeling. At this point, don't try to push away the thoughts or explore them further; just let them float along.

3. Fish out your negative thoughts and find the story

Now that you have an idea of the pattern your thoughts run in, identify the negative ones and start to tackle them one by one. These introspections may lead you to blame yourself, compare yourself to others, or even make you feel hopeless. Dealing with one at a time will allow you to focus on the process and help you avoid being overwhelmed.

For each negative thought, ask yourself these questions:

- What is the trigger for this thought? Is it a certain person, place, or situation?
- Why do I think this? Is there any evidence supporting it?
- What's the root cause of this?
- How do I feel when I think about this? How would I label this thought?
- How do I react to this idea? Do I have a physical reaction to this thought?
- How do I behave as a result of this belief?

4. Take charge of your story

The best way to handle negative thoughts is to treat them like a science experiment—observe them from an objective point of view, be curious, and ask questions. Once you've identified a negative thought and labeled it, don't let it keep going. Instead, bring it back, ask more questions, and gently challenge it.

Is it a rational thought? Is there any evidence to support the thought? Why should you believe it? Asking these questions helps to break the cycle; answering them rationally helps to positively reframe those thoughts. It is important to repeat this process as often as possible.

5. Step out of your mind

You've done a great job so far in controlling the thoughts in your head. It's time to take the fight outside your mind. Here are some practices to help in the battle to overcome your thoughts:

- **Stress management:** Stress can lead you to think negatively more frequently. Being intentional about managing your stress creates a level playing ground.

- **Practice self-care:** Self-care has a lot of benefits, not least of which is arming yourself to tackle your negative thoughts every day. Self-care can look like keeping a journal, listening to your favorite music, or giving yourself a small treat. Intentionality is key here as well.

- **Practice distraction:** It's easy to get caught up in your mind. Once you notice the tempo of your thoughts getting too wild to control, distract yourself so that you have the mental space to tackle these thoughts. Great ways to distract yourself include going for a walk, spending time with loved ones, taking up a hobby, or listening to music.

These steps work. However, if you don't apply them consistently, I'm afraid you won't see sustained results. They are easy to practice but they require consistency.

Check for Mental Issues That May be Compounding the Problem

One of the reasons I advocate for clear communication for chronic overthinkers is the fact that overthinking could be pointing to an underlying issue. Being an overthinker means you most likely do not feel comfortable sharing your worries with people. It's possible that you have tried to speak to one or two people about it, but you were either shut down or your worries were trivialized by the other person.

Realizing that no one understands what you're going through may make you feel defective or broken in some fundamental way. That's far from the truth, but you may in fact be dealing with a mental health issue that's making it difficult for you to overcome overthinking on your own.

Overthinking can be a symptom of several mental health disorders, which will be explored here. It might be easy for you to trace the origin of your overthinking to a particular event or period in your life, or you might realize that you've always been like this.

Either way, finding out if your overthinking could be linked to a mental health issue is essential. Your new life depends on it. I'd like to state here that there should be no shame whatsoever associated with mental illnesses. Nobody makes you feel bad when your body is ill, so why should you feel shame if your mind is? If your overthinking is in fact a symptom of a mental health issue, treating that problem is a surefire way to manage the overthinking.

You might even come to realize that other symptoms you never noticed start to get resolved as well.

- **Low self-esteem**

Having low self-esteem shouldn't be classified as a mental health disorder (and it isn't), but it's serious enough to affect your life negatively. Overthinking can be intricately linked with low self-esteem. Having negative and critical thoughts about yourself, doubting your own strength, and shying away from challenging situations because you don't believe in yourself screams low self-esteem. This frequently spills over into your relationship with your spouse and others. The truth is, everyone around you suffers, not just you. The ironic thing is that avoiding challenging situations reinforces the idea that you're not strong or capable enough. Building your self-love and self-compassion is a good way to raise your self-esteem.

- **Post-traumatic stress disorder (PTSD)**

Overthinking as a trauma response to PTSD deserves proper attention from a professional. Sometimes, you might not recall experiencing a traumatic event, but you might have symptoms that point to PTSD anyway.

Experiencing a traumatic event can change a lot for you. If you find yourself being hyperaware of your environment, having flashbacks about the event or related events, having trouble sleeping, and constantly ruminating about potential dangers, or the likelihood of another traumatic event, you're likely suffering from PTSD and need to seek help from a professional.

- **Anxiety**

Anxiety disorders are mental disturbances characterized by excessive worrying. It's normal to feel anxious about important events, public speaking, and stuff like that, but when you're unable to function normally because of anxiety, it becomes a problem.

If you find yourself having extremely anxiety in reaction to certain events or emotions and you can't really control how you respond to certain situations, you might have an anxiety condition. It's nothing to be worried about—it can be managed. You're more likely to have an anxiety disorder if you've witnessed a traumatic event or you have a shy, inhibited personality type.

Anxiety disturbances can also be inherited because a family history of anxiety can increase your likelihood of getting one. Some thyroid conditions have also been associated with this disorder (Siegmann et al., 2018). Dry mouth, palpitations, difficulty in breathing, and nausea are some common symptoms.

- **Depression**

Depression and overthinking go hand in hand. Overthinking is both a common symptom of and a major risk factor for depression (Nguyen et al., 2019; Michl et al., 2013). This means that it's entirely possible to get depressed if you're an overthinker, or to overthink because you are depressed. We can't really say which causes which, but overthinking has been associated with stress, anxiety, and depression.

Other common symptoms of depression are feeling hopeless or helpless, sleeping a lot or not being able to sleep, and unusual anger or irritability, among others. Cognitive-behavioral therapy (CBT) can help with depression. Some medications, prescribed by a psychiatrist, can also help you feel better.

- **Obsessive-compulsive disorder (OCD)**

Overthinking as a result of OCD will look like having many uncontrollable thoughts which are the object of your obsession. These thoughts will lead to you carrying out habitual, repetitive behaviors that you feel compelled to do. People with OCD cannot control their thoughts or behaviors even when they know that they're being excessive. They also do not derive any pleasure in their compulsive behaviors, although they spend a considerable amount of time each day entertaining their thoughts and acting on their compulsions (NIMH, 2020).

Wrapping Up

Sometimes there's more to your overthinking than meets the eye. It's worthwhile getting any potential mental health issues checked out to rule out any underlying causes of your overthinking. I can feel you wondering why this seems so complex, but I can tell you that whatever's worth doing at all is worth doing well. Don't give up—you can do this.

A huge consequence of overthinking for relationships is lots of arguments, the silent treatment, and fights. What if you could sort those problems out without too much fuss? What if there was a way to argue with your spouse productively? The next chapter will tell you all about how to do that.

Your Quick Workbook

Is there anyone you can confide in when you're feeling overwhelmed by your thoughts and emotions?

_____
_____
_____
_____

Is there a thought that keeps coming up? Have you noticed a particular pattern of thought that appears over and over again?

_____
_____
_____
_____
_____
_____

Based on this chapter, what activities do you think you can engage in to distract you from these thought patterns?

_____

_____

_____

_____

_____

_____

CHAPTER 4

SOLVING CONFLICTS QUICKLY: A HACK

"Whenever you're in conflict with someone, there is one factor that can make the difference between damaging your relationship and deepening it. That factor is attitude."

—William James

Conflict is an unavoidable constant in every relationship. Many people think that the presence or absence of conflict in relationships determines how long the relationship will last and if the couple is really happy. That's a common misconception people fall into, especially overthinkers. I've spoken to people who tend to devolve into intense episodes of overthinking after a disagreement with their partners. This, of course, leads to withdrawal, reduced communication, and further decay in the relationship. It's not surprising to see such relationships soon come to an end.

Interestingly, research has shown that conflict is common in intimate relationships and that the more intimate the relationship is, the higher the tendency to disagree. However, the health of a relationship is better judged by the method of conflict resolution (Moland, 2011).

Truth be told, discord can be stressful. Studies show that it's associated with increased stress, anger, and the flight/fight response. This naturally leads to an increase in blood pressure. Repeated conflict can also lead to apprehension and anxiety in both partners. As you can probably surmise, conflict makes overthinking worse, which, along with anxiety, can lead to depression. On the whole, conflict can affect the stability of the relationship and leave both partners feeling isolated (Laursen, 2010).

On the flip side, conflict can also be good—even healthy—because it helps the two of you learn how to settle differences and become open to contrasting points of view. You'll also learn to be more considerate, and you'll develop your listening and understanding skills. Disagreeing can promote constructive dialogue in your relationship, which leads to intellectual growth and improved mental health. The catch here is that both partners must be allowed to express themselves in a considerate manner during the conflict.

I guess we could say that conflict is both good and bad. So what's the truth here? It's simple. The issue is not conflict itself, but rather the manner in which conflict is approached (i.e., your attitude towards it). This is a huge determinant of its effect on the relationship. While it's possible to have both the right attitude and the wrong attitude towards conflict, your goal should be to foster the right attitude, so let's start with that.

The Right Attitude Towards Relationship Conflict

Having the right attitude towards conflict and its resolution is everything. But I'd be doing you a disservice if I jumped right into that without talking about *you* first.

Yes, you.

You see, developing the right attitude towards conflict resolution depends on your self-perception. Do you love yourself enough? Can you forgive yourself for your mistakes? What's your attitude towards yourself during your inner conflicts? Are you harsh and critical of yourself? You might get away with hiding your true feelings and reactions from other people, but it'll be next to impossible to do so with your significant other. The fact remains that your internal orientation affects your external world, even in conflict resolution.

The first step to resolving conflict begins with you. Examine yourself to find the areas you need to work on. Would you benefit from more self-compassion? Do you practice self-forgiveness? Do you believe that you're deserving of real happiness and support? Are you really in tune with your feelings, or are you avoiding them? Would you rather lash out to hurt someone before they can hurt you?

I admit that it's a lot of work and there's a great deal of self-reflection to be done. Reflecting on these questions while journaling is a great way to dig deep for self-evaluation. The good news is that you don't have to do it all in one day. You can incorporate it into your morning routine and tackle these questions bit by bit.

In the process of doing this, it's natural for more questions to come up. Answer them as best you can and discuss with your partner as well if you need to. Getting your internal mind space in order and checking in with yourself is the key to breaking the cycle of frustrating arguments that end in a deadlock. As you keep doing the internal work, you'll begin to appreciate the differences in your interactions with your partner.

However, keep in mind that adopting the right attitude for conflict resolution in your relationship shouldn't come into play only when you're having an argument. Rather, you have to be ready with the right attitude at all times. Recalibrating your attitude for conflict resolution spills over into other aspects of your relationship and will improve your partnership over time.

The following steps will help you develop the attitude you need for success:

- **Remember that you care about your partner and the relationship.**

You're committed to resolving these issues because you care—why else would you be there?

- **Take a step back to look at the bigger picture.**

How important is the topic you're arguing about in the grand scheme of things? Could your actions have contributed to this conflict? Instead of getting swept up in your feelings, thoughts, and reactions, consider your significant other's feelings, as well as their effort and commitment to the relationship.

- **Be honest at all times.**

However, note that being honest doesn't call for blunt, harsh words. Instead, be tactful and consider your partner's feelings while being as honest as possible.

- **Swallow your pride.**

Someone once said, "Pride builds walls between people while humility builds bridges." When pride creeps into your interactions with your partner, it distorts your perception of the relationship and robs you of the chance to be vulnerable with them. Apologizing first might be hard, but sometimes it's necessary. Are you holding on to pride in ways that are damaging your relationship?

- **Remember what the fight is really about.**

The biggest mistake couples often make is to assume that conflict means they're pitted against each other. That's the farthest thing from the truth. Conflict should be about you and your partner working as a team against the issue in question. Adopting an "us vs. them" mentality is a life-changing step for your relationship. Treat your significant other with compassion at all times because they're on your team. Forgive easily and often.

- **Show respect.**

Respecting your significant other means always being considerate of them and never demeaning them or making them feel less-than.

The Wrong Attitude Towards Relationship Conflict

I think we can both agree here that conflict is practically inevitable and can even be healthy. For the most part, when you have an argument with your partner, you're probably not doing it to end the relationship; instead, you're probably trying to express yourself and your feelings. But the sad truth is that poorly handled conflict that occurs over and over again can lead to an abrupt end to the relationship. If you find that each confrontation with your partner ends in cold silence, frustration, and distance, then you need to check your attitude towards confrontation. You might be making one of these mistakes:

- **You're not expressing yourself often enough.**

Sometimes keeping quiet because you don't want to stir things up isn't the best way to go. In fact, I daresay it's not the way to go at all. Bottling things up because you're scared of the relationship ending or because you'd rather avoid things getting messy leads to resentment, doubt, anger, and unhappiness.

It might seem like the easy way out, but it eventually becomes stressful when you finally let your feelings out. And make no mistake, these feelings will come out, one way or another. So if you're reading this and thinking, "Well, thank goodness I don't argue much with my partner, and I'd rather eat my hat than start or entertain a fight, so I'm good to go"—I regret to tell you (okay, I don't really regret it) that you're most definitely *not* good to go. That fight you're avoiding will still happen, but it'll be bigger, messier, and more stressful.

Make a decision to communicate with your partner today. If an issue is still on your mind a full 48 hours after it occurs, then you need to talk it out. Thankfully, with the tips I've given you in the previous section, you should be able to do that.

- **You're always on the defensive.**

If you always have to be right in every argument, you have a certain idea of how things should be done, you're quick to jump to your own defense, or you're convinced that you're never the problem in the relationship, there's a very big possibility that your defensive attitude is a source of frustration for your partner.

While it might even be true that you're right most of the time, there's more than one way to be right. Rather than pointing out the 50 ways that you're right, slow down to listen to your partner and consider their point of view. If you're constantly on the defensive, your significant other will feel unheard, isolated, and resentful. You need to quit criticizing and blaming your partner whenever you feel attacked.

- **You're fond of overgeneralizing.**

As an overthinker, it's easy to judge your partner based on their actions and connect said actions to other previous actions. Then you'll find yourself associating them with certain behavior and overgeneralizing. Statements that start with "You always…" or "You never…" should be avoided, especially in the heat of an argument.

If you've noticed a pattern of behavior in your partner, rather than bringing it up while you're arguing and emotions are running high, save it for a later date when you're both calm. Don't bring up past incidents to aggravate current issues.

- **You're quite the mind-reader.**

I'm sure there have been incidents where you analyzed your partner's actions and just "knew" what their intentions were while carrying out those actions. Throw in a healthy dose of speculation and negative thoughts, and *voila!*—you have a relationship headed for the rocks. To be honest, a good amount of conflict could be avoided by simply asking questions and clarifying matters with your partner. I encourage you to, as the popular saying goes, "Assume nothing and question everything."

- **You don't listen.**

Sure, you're present with your partner and you spend as much time as possible with them, but do you listen? I mean, *really* listen. Do you roll your eyes, look at your phone screen, or watch the game while your spouse is trying to tell you something important? Or perhaps you spend that time rehearsing your next debate point in your head instead of listening? These are classic signs of a poor listener.

Why not try active listening? Eliminate distractions whenever you're spending time with your partner. Put the phone or book down, turn off the TV for a moment. You get the idea. Practice mindfulness when you're spending time with your significant other. Ask questions and clarify their statements. This might seem like a trivial tip, but it goes a long way.

- **You're the Ice King/Queen.**

If you're quick to ice out your partner after an argument, or even before an impending argument, you're gravely reducing your chances of settling your disputes amicably. Refusing to discuss a particular issue or even listen to your spouse when they're willing to talk about it shows disrespect and a lack of consideration on your part.

- **You keep withholding your love.**

Treating your partner unkindly after a disagreement is an alarming sign of deterioration in your relationship. Withdrawing your love and affection might seem like a good way to communicate your displeasure, but all it does is drive the wedge between yourself and your spouse deeper.

Maintaining a relationship takes a lot of work, but the best part is that the rewards are plentiful too. If you're guilty of any of these practices, taking intentional steps to change them will improve the quality of your relationship, and you'll see the positive impact almost immediately.

Why Conflicts Should be Resolved in a Timely Manner

What's the silliest thing you've ever argued about? The answers I've heard range from leaving the toilet seat up to chewing noisily in public. I'm sure there are even sillier things you've probably argued about. It's weird, but these petty arguments are often the most annoying ones ever!

Now I want you to think about the *worst* argument you've had with your partner. I mean the biggest knock-down drag-out fight you've experienced. What was it about? How did you resolve it? Was it even truly resolved? How did it affect your relationship?

Study the patterns of both types of arguments—the silly ones and the serious ones. What is the difference between them? How did they start and how were they resolved? It's likely that the silly arguments were never fully resolved; you probably still argue about leaving the toilet seat up or leaving clothes on the floor instead of tossing them into the laundry basket. And that's okay. Some conflicts will never be fully resolved, especially between two people who spend a lot of time together. The key to conflict resolution here is picking your battles wisely.

One big mistake a lot of people make with major conflicts is avoiding the topic and walking on eggshells around each other, hoping that it'll die down. Often, couples like that are likely to go on to have several big arguments revolving around that one elephant in the room. This is because they've missed what is perhaps the most important factor in positive conflict resolution: timing. Resolving the conflict at the best time possible may very well be the key to the health of your relationship.

This might sound unconventional, but there are three possible best times for conflict resolution: before it starts, during the conflict, and after the conflict. Preventing confrontation is the best option, in my opinion. Having a strong bond of friendship and positivity is the key to preventing conflicts before they arise. Showing consistent affection for each other builds up a store of positivity, which helps buffet the relationship during times of conflict.

The next best time to resolve a conflict is during the conflict itself. This requires a strong bond of friendship, communication, and intuition. It will help both of you realize when the argument has become unproductive, which is the minute that the quarrel devolves into other issues that are not connected to the original problem.

You may also notice when the quarrel becomes more about protecting your egos than honest communication. At this point, it's essential to take a small break to figure out where you lost the plot. Then you should reconvene and discuss the matter with the end goal of compromise and preservation in mind.

However, as lovely as resolving conflict before it starts or right in the middle of it sounds, the truth is most of us miss that ship and watch it sail far, far away. This means that the most practical time for conflict resolution, for most people, is after said conflict. This requires striking a delicate balance because attempting to resolve it too soon may lead to further quarrels while waiting too long leads to a buildup of negative emotions and complications.

Conflict is usually accompanied by raw emotions like anger, resentment, and even pain. Attempting to talk to your partner in this state is, at best, unproductive. Letting disputes go unresolved for long periods of time warps the initial negative emotions, and they grow into something ugly and messy. The simple rule of thumb is: the longer conflict is left unchecked, the more difficult it is to actually resolve.

An acceptable time to settle a conflict could be as little as 30 minutes after the conflict to as much as two days after. This is because some distance to process the event is needed. Proper processing of the argument helps both partners cool off, evaluate their emotions, and put things in perspective. As always, different strokes work for different folks, but the bottom line is that conflicts should be resolved as soon as possible after both partners have processed the quarrel.

How to Handle Conflict and Prevent Communication Breaches

If you've not been living under some rock, you've probably heard of Noah and Allie's love story in *The Notebook*. Their love was so passionate and strong that even after 14 years, just as Allie was about to marry someone else, she found Noah, fell in love with him again, and eventually married him.

If you don't know what I'm talking about, *The Notebook* is a book written by Nicholas Sparks which was later adapted into a movie. In the movie, I noticed that Noah and Allie constantly quarreled. They couldn't agree on practically anything, yet their love was so strong that after they got married, they lived happily together for 60 years until Allie got Alzheimer's disease and forgot her husband and family. So Noah did the most romantic thing possible: he wrote a notebook filled with their stories and memories and read it to her each day. Heartwarming, right? I digress.

Back to their constant conflict. One reason they fought a lot was because they were from different backgrounds; another reason is that Noah could have communicated with Allie more respectfully. So why did they still get back together if they couldn't go very long without arguing? My opinion is that they were willing to communicate, and they always kept their love at the forefront of the union.

Of course, you're free to disagree, but the biggest lesson for me from the book was that constant communication and a mutual determination to see your love through to the end can bring the refreshing rays of the sun back to any dark, dead relationship. (A fun fact about this story is that it is based on the true story of a couple the author once met.)

As with anything, communication can be ineffective or effective. It's important to note that communication will look different for different couples because it's largely based on personality types as well as personal differences. The bottom line is that effective and positive communication is the key to sustaining happy relationships for the long term (Tomuletiu et al., 2014).

Before we look at the keys to effective communication, how do you know whether or not you're communicating effectively with your partner? Here are four important signs of poor communication.

- **Your squabbles become big fights.**

Your arguments may often start small, but then the focus switches quickly from one issue to another. For example, an inconsequential fight over leaving the laundry on the floor can quickly become a messy, emotional argument about how one partner is too controlling or always nags, and then it can go quickly into how annoying and lazy the other partner is, and… KA-BOOM!

- **You never acknowledge or validate each other's feelings.**

Picture a scene where you're telling your partner that you didn't like the way they talked down to you at a gathering with mutual friends. How would you feel if they responded by saying that they never talk down to you and that you're being too sensitive and self-conscious, and they refuse to see your point of view? I'm not a betting man, but I'm sure you'd leave that conversation feeling unheard, annoyed, and maybe even resentful. You don't need to be psychic to know that these unresolved negative feelings will be turning up at the next argument like a bad coin.

- **You're quick to attribute negative intentions to your partner's words and behaviors.**

If you find yourselves ascribing negative meaning to each other's actions, your communication might be going down the drain. For example, if you notice that your partner forgets to buy an appropriate gift for your anniversary, you may conclude that they're cheating on you or that they don't care about your union anymore. Humans are naturally inclined to confirmation bias, so you'll start to look for more evidence to support this claim and most likely start to make wrong connections, which leads to things being blown out of proportion.

- **You're withdrawing from or avoiding each other.**

This is a critical sign in any relationship and should be fixed as soon as possible. Avoiding each other's company and refusing to discuss intimate matters or topics of dissension leads to feelings of emotional and physical loneliness. This can cause one partner to seek an emotional or physical connection outside the partnership. I'm sure we can agree that this is the beginning of a very slippery slope.

If you can identify with any of these signs or you find that your communication patterns with your spouse are getting dangerously close to any of these situations, then you need to fix it—and quickly.

Here are a few ways to fix the communication in your relationship. These steps are also useful if you'd like to improve the quality of your communication:

- **Take stock of your feelings first.**

Are you satisfied with where your relationship is today? Do you think you could improve your communication? How do you feel about the relationship? This step can also be used right before an argument. Are you too angry or emotional to make a rational decision right now? Take a step back to process those emotions before discussing any issue. Ask for a timeout and go for a walk or listen to some music to help you calm down.

- **Understand your partner.**

Talk to your partner about their opinions on communicating effectively. What does it look like for them? How do they feel about it? Are they satisfied with the current contact level? What's their communication style (are they timid, assertive, passive-aggressive, avoidant)? What's yours? Talk about how this affects your relationship.

- **Settle previously unresolved issues.**

This might sound like you're borrowing trouble, but bringing these issues to light, especially if they're still bothering you or your partner, helps to wipe the slate clean. Conflict is typically weighed down by previous unresolved issues, which tends to muddy the waters and make resolution of current issues next to impossible.

- **Timing is everything.**

Carefully consider the best time to bring up an issue. Don't ambush your spouse by springing the conflict on them. Informing your partner ahead of time helps them prepare for the discussion and feel less defensive.

- **Begin your sentences with "I."**

This helps to shift the focus from accusation ("You always/never…") to talking about your feelings. Your spouse is much more likely to respond positively if you tell them how their actions have affected you.

- **Focus on listening and being heard.**

Communicate your points to your significant other in clear, concise statements that are not accusatory. When they're speaking, give them your full attention and process what they've said rather than using that time to think of a reply. Pay attention to your body language as well as your partner's body language. Nodding when they speak, having an encouraging expression, putting down your phone, and even lightly stroking their arm are all great ways to communicate nonverbally with your partner.

- **Switch your focus to compromise and resolution rather than winning.**

Once you're determined to have your argument end in a peaceful resolution, it becomes much easier to compromise.

- **Establish healthy boundaries.**

Boundaries make a relationship healthier, and they are essential for proper communication. Examples could be agreeing not to use sarcastic or hurtful words when communicating or deciding to take a timeout when things get heated. Find what works for your relationship and keep exploring new methods as you progress.

- **Keep in touch.**

Update your partner at different times during your day via text or calls. These regular check-ins might seem mundane, but they help to build a habit of sustained communication and deepen intimacy.

Wrapping Up

It's such a relief to find out that having a fight or two isn't the end of the world, isn't it? Even if you're skeptical about what you just read, take my word for it—it works. Let me know how it goes!

Now, we've talked a lot about you, but we both know that it takes two to tango in every relationship. Let's look at your partner; how does your overthinking affect them, and how can you make sure they come along in your process of improvement? I'll tell you all about this in the next chapter.

Your Quick Workbook

How does being in a conflict with your partner make you feel?

_____

_____

_____

_____

_____

Do you think your past conflicts with your partner have strengthened or harmed your relationship with each other?

_____

_____

_____

_____

_____

_____

Do you agree that your communication with your partner needs to be worked on?

_____

_____

_____

_____

_____

If you haven't been managing your conflicts effectively up till now, do you think what you learned in this chapter can help you manage your conflicts better?

_____

_____

_____

_____

_____

CHAPTER 5

HOW TO PRIORITIZE HEALTHY COMMUNICATION OVER OVERTHINKING

"Be devoted to one another in love. Honor one another above yourselves."

—Romans 12:10

I once had a friend who gave her husband the silent treatment for a week. She was annoyed that he didn't get her a nice gift for their anniversary, just a gift card. Sure, she made dinner, but she rarely talked at the table. She'd go to bed before him and wake up earlier than usual so she didn't have to talk to him.

When they visited me, she made an offhand comment about how marriage could be difficult sometimes. I probed further as to why she said that, and she told me to direct my question to her husband. When I asked him, he said, "I don't know what she's talking about; it's been a great week for me. So much peace and calmness for the first time in a long while."

His wife was stunned. She said, "But I was giving you the silent treatment!"

He said, "Oh, that's what that was? I'd like to order more silent treatment in that case."

We all had a good laugh about it. I encouraged her to get better at expressing her desires.

—**Sophia**

Respecting Your Partner's Struggles and Personal Issues

I'm sure you'll agree that there's no perfect relationship out there. This sounds like a cliché, but acknowledging and accepting this fact is important, especially if you tend to overthink. You might find yourself feeling anxious about the health of your connection and maybe comparing your partnership to another, seemingly more successful one. But I want you to know that comparison will only steal your joy, and no one really has it figured out. Instead of worrying and comparing, why not focus on what you can control? Why not work to make your relationship better? I think that's the best way to go, don't you?

When it comes to maintaining relationships and working to transform them into healthy ones, one of the most overlooked components for success is respect. It can be quite easy to get so caught up in your own emotions, struggles, and desires that you fail to realize that your partner has those too. This is especially true when there's constant conflict in the partnership. Being intentional about respecting your partner builds the relationship and helps you observe the tiny, intricate details that you might have missed. It helps you recognize that your partner is a person with their own concerns and struggles.

Before you go further, evaluate the current state of the relationship and ask yourself a few questions. You should involve your partner in this exercise as much as possible. These questions are a great place to start:

- What does respect mean to you? What does it mean to your partner?
- Do your expectations look different from your partner's? If so, how do you plan to manage the differences?
- Do you have boundaries in your relationship? Does your partner have boundaries, and do they recognize your boundaries?
- Do you trust your spouse? Can you open up about your feelings and emotions to them?
- Can they trust you to do the same?
- What are clear signs of respect and disrespect for the two of you?
- What is the next step to take if someone feels disrespected?

These questions will help you and your partner start a conversation that should never stop and help you to be cognizant of your other half as a person who needs a safe space to be vulnerable and express themselves.

A big part of respect is being accountable for your actions and their consequences. Realize that sometimes you might unknowingly offend your partner or cross their boundaries. Your actions may hurt your partner. Instead of shifting blame or justifying your actions, why not try apologizing and working with them to see how to avoid future occurrences? Start the habit of daily, weekly, and monthly check-ins. Discuss the heavy stuff, be unflinchingly honest, and reaffirm your commitment to each other.

Once you realize that respect and trust are two sides of the same coin, you'll be less likely to clash with your partner over minor issues. If you trust that they're committed to you, then you should respect them by not looking through their phone, for example, or following them whenever they're out.

A few people I've talked to who have considered this idea came to the realization that they didn't trust their partner. If you're not sure whether or not you trust your partner, then you have to start the journey to rebuilding trust. Trust me, your relationship will be much better for it.

Self-Talk to Remind Yourself That It Takes Two to Tango

"Love is a two-way street constantly under construction."

—Carroll Bryant

A lot of people enter relationships with an idea of what their ideal relationship looks like. They come in with set expectations and often find something entirely different than what they expected. One question to ask yourself here is: What forms the basis of your expectations for your relationships?

Oftentimes we form our expectations for romantic partnerships from different sources. They could come from seeing our parents' bond while growing up, or they could come from movies, books, or even culture. Remember that you and your partner are two different people from two different backgrounds with distinct ideas of what your connection should look like, and this needs to be acknowledged and discussed if you want to make any progress in improving the relationship.

The unfortunate part is that when a new romantic relationship starts, because of all the gooey emotions and the feel-good hormones running amok, we often do not take enough time to compare our expectations for the relationship with our partner's, and instead cruise along on the sea of newfound love. I don't know about you, but I think that is a recipe for disaster. Thankfully, most couples are able to balance out their expectations and adjust to the real work of building a life together eventually. But success here depends on a host of factors. The bottom line remains that at some point in your relationship, a reorientation must take place involving both parties for the stability of the partnership.

Now that we've established that we have two different people working together to form one harmonious union, what can you do to reorient your expectations and achieve a deeper, more intimate relationship with your partner? The truth is, you can't go this route alone; your partner needs to be equally committed to the growth and success of the relationship.

As always, the first thing to do is to evaluate yourself. What do you think of yourself? What's that inner voice telling you about yourself and about your relationship? Why is it saying that? I've said this before, but it bears repeating: a positive inner attitude makes it easier to give and receive love. If you have the right amount of self-love and you practice self-compassion frequently, you'll find it easier to extend the same level of love and compassion to your partner as well as to receive love and deep intimacy from them in return.

The work of evaluating yourself isn't something you can accomplish in five minutes; rather, it is an ongoing process that requires your intentional consistency. More often than not, you'll find that your inner voice is sorely lacking in compassion and self-love. The best way to tackle that is to recalibrate and challenge your inner self to advocate for the good of your relationship. The best way to do this is through positive self-talk.

Positive self-talk conditions your mind to accept new facts. The idea of talking your way from a negative mindset to a positive one might sound farfetched or even crazy, but I'm here to tell you that it's entirely possible.

Self-talk is an often-underutilized tool to improve or save your relationship. In fact, using the right self-talk can revitalize your outlook on all your relationships, not just your relationship with your spouse. This simple framework is a great way to identify and recalibrate your negative thoughts and ruminations.

- What am I telling myself?
- What's the root cause of these thoughts?
- Are they helpful thoughts?
- What can I tell myself to overcome this?
- What can I do to overcome this?

For example, let's say you notice that your partner has been distracted recently, keeps coming home late from work, and isn't volunteering to spend time with you unless you ask. Your overthinking brain naturally suspects that they're getting tired of the relationship at best, or maybe even seeing someone else at worst. Using the framework above can help you change your self-talk, and I'll show you how:

- What am I telling myself? "My partner is probably cheating on me because they're tired of the relationship and probably don't love me anymore."

- What's the root cause of these thoughts? "I heard that Shirley and Tom got a divorce. Tom is very good friends with my partner and might have influenced them to look for someone better. I don't think I'm good enough for this relationship."
- Is this thought helpful? "No."
- What can I tell myself to overcome this? "I remember my partner mentioning that a promotion process at work is coming up, so they might be stressed about that."
- What can I do to overcome this? "I can ask my partner about work and offer comfort by running them a bath or offering them a massage. I can then gently express my fears to them."

Self-talk goes a long way to correct negative assumptions about ourselves or our spouses that may not be correct. Without proper evaluation and recalibration, it becomes easy to move from having these unhelpful thoughts to feeling emotions like resentment, anger, jealousy, or self-pity. Positive self-talk helps you become receptive and empathetic towards yourself, your spouse, and others.

Avoiding Self-Centeredness and Asking What Your Partner Needs

This might be difficult for you to admit, but your partner may have accused you of being selfish and now you can't help seeing all the different scenarios that point to it as the truth. Are you really self-centered?

It's possible that you haven't ever considered the fact that you could be self-centered in your relationship. If your partner doesn't complain about it, then everything is good on that front, right? Maybe, maybe not.

Being self-centered means you're more likely to make decisions that favor yourself over those that are more beneficial for the good of your relationship. If you don't consider your significant other while making big decisions or you do things that hurt them, even though you're aware that they don't like it, you might be more selfish than you thought.

In a relationship, if one partner is shy and introverted or the other partner is more aggressive and dominant, it's likely that someone's needs are being overlooked in favor of the other person. In a relationship with two self-centered people, there's a noticeable lack of intimacy and communication. Being self-centered will cause feelings of dissatisfaction, isolation, and resentment in your partner.

The first step in solving this issue is to evaluate yourself and your actions in the relationship. These questions might help:

- Are my actions selfish?
- Do I have a habit of putting myself first?

- Do I naturally expect my partner to do things that please me?
- Do I take time out to pay attention to my partner?
- Has my partner ever accused me of being self-centered?
- Do I give my partner the freedom to grow and express themselves in the relationship?
- Do I feel threatened when my partner spends time with friends and loved ones?
- Would I say that I'm possessive?

Reflecting on these questions and writing down the answers will help you gauge how self-centered you actually are.

The next step is to talk to your partner. Ask them what they think and listen to their honest opinion. If they say that they do think you're selfish, don't panic. Admitting that there's a problem is the first step to solving it. Look back on the behaviors your partner points out and try to find out why you might have acted that way. Intentionally decide to take steps to become less self-centered.

Here are a few tips that will help you become less self-oriented and more committed to the growth of your relationship. As always, being consistent and intentional is necessary.

- **Pay close attention to your partner.**

How often do you really listen to them? Are you meeting their needs? Try to talk to them about their feelings, wants, and needs. Ask for their opinions. A great way to put your partner first is to put yourself in their shoes. Think about what you would want them to do for you and then do the same thing for them.

- **Realize that your partner has a life outside of you.**

If you're being self-centered in your relationship, it's easy to assume your partner's whole world revolves around you. If you find yourself constantly expecting your partner to drop everything to cater to your needs, or you don't mind that they do things for you all the time and you don't reciprocate these gestures, take a step back and think about your partner. Understanding that your partner has a life outside of your relationship is important, as it will help to prevent conflict and help you become more considerate.

- **Be willing to compromise.**

You might be used to getting your own way in your relationship, especially if you feel like you have a more important job or you're somehow the more important person in the relationship. Learning to humble yourself and consciously compromise with your partner is a great way to avoid self-centeredness.

- **Take your ego out of the equation.**

Entertaining your pride will only make you defend your selfish behavior. Instead, pay attention to the fact that your partner deserves to feel safe being vulnerable with you.

- **Cultivate the habit of generosity.**

Learning how to give is a great way to combat self-centeredness. Deliberately decide to be generous with your time, your attention, your words, and your presence in your relationship to make your partner feel special and loved.

- **Support and celebrate your partner.**

If you've become a self-centered person in your relationship, it might be normal for you to forget important anniversaries and events. Making a deliberate attempt to keep track of these days and commemorate them is a great way to make your spouse feel loved and special. Participating in your partner's interests, encouraging them when they're feeling discouraged, and taking time to be present as much as possible are also helpful.

This is not an exhaustive list of ways to curb self-centeredness in your relationship, but these tips will certainly help. As you start implementing these actions, you'll discover even more ways to make your partner feel loved and strengthen your relationship.

How to Cultivate Trust and Avoid Paranoia

Trust is the bedrock of a healthy relationship. Overthinkers tend to have trust issues with their partners, which are worsened if they have experienced traumatic past relationships. These issues might come up in different ways. Recognizing that you do not trust your partner is just the first step to rebuilding confidence. It's not possible to have a long-lasting relationship without trust.

Being able to rely on your partner helps you feel safe and builds intimacy in your relationship. You'll find that you feel free to be as vulnerable and natural as you want because you're sure that your partner is looking out for you no matter what. Trust also helps to minimize conflict; it provides the element of security that is needed in every loving relationship.

Saying that you trust someone means you believe they are reliable and honest. It means you know you're able to depend on them because they have integrity and are faithful to you. On the other hand, here are some of the signs that you don't trust your partner.

- **You assume the worst.**

You find it easy to ascribe the worst possible meaning to your partner's behaviors and intentions, even when they have shown themselves to be reliable in the past.

- **You're constantly suspicious.**

You're always suspicious that your partner is doing something to hurt you in some way.

- **You don't forgive easily.**

When you have trust issues, moving on from past hurts might be very difficult for you. This can affect all aspects of your life and color your interactions with your significant other as well as your family and friends.

- **You keep a distance between yourself and others.**

People with trust issues typically separate themselves from other people and do not let themselves experience true intimacy in a relationship, often because they're afraid of being betrayed or disappointed.

- **You focus on the negative.**

Even though you might have evidence to the contrary, you're more focused on all the things that could go wrong in your relationship and are quick to point out your partner's flaws and weaknesses rather than focusing on their good qualities.

Having trust issues can leave both you and your spouse feeling misunderstood, isolated, and unloved. A lack of trust might be an indicator that your relationship is in distress. In that case, you need to work to rebuild the trust or to solve your trust issues with your partner. To do this, here are some action steps:

- **Prioritize building trust.**

This can look like slowly letting your spouse deeper into your life and having faith in their words, actions, and intentions. It's important to know that as you build confidence with your partner, you must be ready to forgive because mistakes are bound to happen.

- **Trust yourself.**

The best way to trust others is to trust yourself first. Developing a strong sense of self-awareness can help you evaluate other people and interact with them in a more positive way. The fact is, learning how to trust yourself is like a muscle that can be developed with practice, just like all the other muscles in the body.

The ability to forgive yourself must go hand-in-hand with the ability to trust or else you'll end up doing more damage than good.

If you find yourself excessively concerned with monitoring your partner's movements, doubting their intentions, or misjudging their actions, it's possible you're experiencing some paranoia about your relationship. Here's a list of quick tips for tackling paranoia.

1. Identify the reason you're feeling paranoid

Has your partner given you any reason to distrust them in the past? Are you acting this way based on an experience in a previous relationship? Identifying the cause of your paranoia will help you to think more rationally about it.

2. Eliminate stress

Stress is a very common cause of paranoia. Practicing relaxation techniques can help you overcome stress.

3. Practice self-care

A good way to eliminate paranoia is to take time out of your day to practice self-care, even if it's something as simple as a minute or two of deep breathing or a quick walk around the block.

4. Share your fears with your partner

Oftentimes, no matter how much you try to rationalize and counteract the feelings of paranoia, the best and most efficient way to eliminate these feelings is to discuss your paranoid thoughts with your partner. Explain your struggles and their root cause. Don't be shy to ask for the support you need. Both of you can work out strategies to help put your mind at rest.

The Importance of Taking Your Partner at Their Word

In this chapter so far, we've discussed some of the various aspects of communication in a healthy relationship. You've had to do a lot of self-reflection at different points (if you haven't done the exercises yet, this is your cue to go back and do them!), and I'm sure you're committed to doing the work to improve your relationship. However, this last section is perhaps the most critical yet, as it's about something that could destroy all your progress if you're not cautious.

This might sound cliché, but if you're an overthinker, the best way to develop confidence in your partner and silence those nagging thoughts is to trust them. What better way to develop trust than to actually…trust what they say? Doubting your partner's words can be a sneaky way to maintain contact with your overthinking even after you've promised to cut all ties. It's particularly tempting to entertain anxious thoughts about your partner's statements because it's all in your head—who's going to know if you decide to reexamine and second-guess their words?

However, not believing your partner's word is a surefire way to undermine the trust and intimacy in your relationship. You'll almost certainly find yourself feeling resentful of or apathetic towards your partner at the end of the day. Before you know it, these feelings manifest in your attitude and actions towards your significant other.

The bottom line is this: Trusting your partner enough to accept their words at face value helps you to build trust in your relationship. However, before you trust the words, you might benefit from asking your spouse questions to clarify exactly what they mean. This will help to eliminate any doubt or confusion in your mind and also help to manage your expectations.

Don't be afraid to ask your spouse for what you need, and be as honest and direct as possible. And remember to open up to your partner about your feelings, especially if you're struggling with believing them. This might seem difficult and unnecessary, but it actually helps to deepen the intimacy in your relationship.

Wrapping Up

I know this chapter was particularly hard for you because it probably seemed like I asked you to do everything you'd rather not do. I mean, taking your partner at their word?! I know. It could definitely be difficult. But as uncomfortable as it seems now, you'll be happy with yourself for putting in the work when your relationship starts to flourish.

While communication and trust are very important, I would be remiss if we didn't talk about the other elephant in the room. This guy comes along with overthinking and makes himself comfortable. I'm talking about the negativity in your relationship. It might seem like an abstract concept now, but you'll hear all about it in the next chapter and realize why you need to take it seriously.

Your Quick Workbook

Do you solely take all the blame for the issues in your relationship, put all the blame on your partner, or do you both share the blame?

How receptive are you and your partner to each other's needs?

How would you feel if you found out your partner didn't trust you?

Why do you think you find it hard to trust your partner?

CHAPTER 6

DEALING WITH NEGATIVE ENERGY, THOUGHTS, AND HABITS IN YOUR MARRIAGE

"Cast all your anxiety on him because he cares for you."
—1 Peter 5:7

I'll be the first to admit that relationships can be awfully tricky to navigate. Knowing when to commit fully, having the strength to realize that a relationship isn't serving you anymore, or choosing to take a few steps back from your partner even though you'd rather stay isn't for the faint of heart. Finding a delicate balance between trust and self-awareness is necessary for surviving a relationship that may turn out badly for you.

A friend once told me about this woman who was in a seemingly happy relationship with her partner. They had a whirlwind dating period and soon moved in together. But her friends noticed that she was always drained and that she seemed eager to spend time with her friends rather than go home to her significant other. At first, they were concerned that she was being abused, and they gently asked her if everything was all right. She strongly denied any abuse and said everything was fine.

After gentle, persistent probing, she finally admitted that she just didn't enjoy spending time with her partner anymore. Sure, they were still physically intimate, but that was about the only time they saw eye to eye on anything. She said that they argued all the time, they were not as emotionally intimate as they used to be, and she always felt exhausted whenever she had to be around him. Interestingly, she likened her significant other to an "energy vampire" who drained her every time she was around him.

This description stuck with me even though it's been about seven years since I heard that story. I think it was so compelling because of the vivid way she described the negative energy in her relationship. This might sound odd, but it's possible to be in an intimate relationship with negative energy. You or your partner may be injecting negativity into your union as a result of some previous experience that caused emotional damage.

Recognizing Negative Vibes in Your Relationship

Toxic vibes, or negative energy, is pretty easy to spot from the outside, but strangely it becomes difficult to do so when you're neck-deep in the relationship. When the characteristics of your partnership embody the total opposite of everything a healthy union is meant to be, it's most likely toxic. If you realize that there is no intimacy, that you don't support each other, that there is unhealthy competition and disrespect, then your relationship has officially been overtaken by negative vibes.

These signs point towards negativity in your relationship:

- **Constant fighting**

We've covered the idea that conflict can actually be healthy in a relationship, but being unable to successfully compromise for conflict resolution is a sign of toxicity. Constant arguing illuminates a deeper problem with communication, especially if words of disrespect, insults, and harsh language are involved.

- **Manipulation**

This can look like the silent treatment, withdrawal of affection, or trying to make your partner jealous.

- **Feeling uncomfortable with your partner**

The point of being in a relationship is to experience the peaceful, intimate feeling of being emotionally close to someone you trust. You'll most likely stay in a relationship if being with that person makes you happier than being alone. However, if you notice that you're always feeling nervous and uncomfortable or you experience tension around your partner, that could indicate that your relationship is full of negativity.

- **Constantly complaining about your partner to others**

If you find that you never have anything good to say about your relationship or your spouse to anyone, it's likely that your relationship is a toxic one.

- **No intimacy or affection**

Being physically intimate is a nice perk of a long-term relationship, and it also serves to strengthen the emotional connection between you. Avoiding physical intimacy with your partner might be a sign that there's something negative in the works.

- **Making your friends uncomfortable**

If your relationship has deteriorated to the point where you both take potshots at each other while in public with your friends, it's a surefire sign that toxic vibes have taken over your partnership entirely. This might even cause your friends to start taking sides, which means the bad energy has begun to leak outwards.

If you've noticed that your relationship is full of negative vibes, it might be time to take a step back and evaluate it. Are you sure you want to be in that kind of relationship? What part have you played in creating negativity? You must work to overcome this challenge and transform the bad energy into positive vibes.

Improving Your Self-Esteem to Stay Positive and Kind in Your Marriage

"For you created my inmost being;
you knit me together in my mother's womb.
I praise you because I am fearfully and wonderfully made;
your works are wonderful,

I know that fully well."

—Psalm 139:13–14

One of the most popular phrases relating to self-care and self-love is "you can't pour from an empty cup." We've concluded that loving your partner in the way they deserve to be loved begins with loving yourself. You just can't love someone else fully if you don't love *you*. This is where self-esteem comes into play. Self-esteem is simply the way you perceive yourself, and it's very important for a balanced and satisfying life.

If you had to describe yourself honestly to someone else, what would you say?

Do you feel good about yourself, or do you only have negative things to say? What do you think of yourself? People with low self-esteem may find it difficult to have long-lasting, trusting relationships. They might not want to stand up for themselves and might reject any good thing that comes their way.

Low self-esteem can ruin a union in this way. Conversely, developing healthy self-respect sets the bar for how you'll be treated in your relationship and also guides you on how to treat your partner. It means that you're less likely to become unhealthily attached to each other (codependency) and you're able to sort out your own emotional needs alone. A relationship is all about two people coming together to form one unit, true, but it's often necessary to maintain some degree of independence in your relationship to allow for your own experiences and happiness.

Having low self-regard makes you constantly doubt yourself and believe that you're not good enough, which, in turn, leads you to depend on your spouse for approval, love, and validation. This can be dangerous if you are with an inconsiderate or unstable partner.

So, how can you boost your self-esteem?

- **Focus on yourself.**

It goes without saying that building your self-esteem requires you to spend more time alone. Getting to know and accept yourself is essential. A lot of people find it difficult to spend hours and hours by themselves, but start small and build your way up. Do things that you enjoy, whether that's reading, journaling, listening to music, or pursuing a solo hobby.

- **Claim your space.**

Some degree of independence is needed on your journey to reclaiming your self-esteem. Being in a partnership that completely absorbs your identity and doesn't let you differentiate yourself isn't a sign of undying love; it's an unhealthy move for both you and your partner.

- **Embrace true happiness.**

No one can make you truly happy except yourself. Your partner can only improve whatever level of happiness you've already achieved on your own. Relying on your spouse for a level of emotional responsibility beyond what they can handle can cause an imbalance in your relationship that ends with you trying to take way more than your partner might be ready to give. Being in charge of your own happiness means knowing that happiness is a choice you must make every day.

- **Forgive yourself.**

It's natural to have flaws. No one is perfect. These flaws do not make you a terrible or unlovable person, and you need to recognize that and forgive yourself for past mistakes.

- **See yourself through your partner's eyes.**

Try this out. Ask your spouse to describe how they see you and why they love you. This may sound like you're fishing for cheap compliments, but sometimes, taking note of the small ways in which someone notices how amazing you are is a great way to boost your self-esteem.

- **Find the root cause.**

Low self-esteem can be caused by a variety of factors. Taking the time to find out why you're struggling with low self-esteem is a huge step in the right direction.

- **Keep a journal.**

I'm sure you thought you'd heard the last of me advocating for journals, but here we are again. Keeping a journal gives you a safe space to process your thoughts. It's best to write in your journal every day for at least 10 minutes per day.

Some prompts to get you started are:

- What am I feeling right now?
- Why am I feeling this way?
- How does my partner make me feel?
- How would I like to make my partner feel?
- Are there any problems in my relationship right now?
- How would I like my relationship with my partner to improve?

After writing in your journal, it might be best to discuss some of the things you've discovered with your partner.

Building Compassion and Avoiding Blame

Most people are surprised when I tell them that, for the most part, it's possible to develop any character attributes you want as long as you're ready to put your mind to it. I compare these attributes to muscles in the body, which we all know can get bigger when used more often.

In the same way, practicing particular attributes or characteristics will create a habit that you will soon unconsciously start to follow.

However, just as it's possible to develop positive attributes, it's also fairly easy to develop negative attributes through consistent repetition.

A good example of this is the tendency to blame each other. Let's be honest here, nobody wins at the blame game. All it does is shift blame endlessly from one person to the other. It also intensifies feelings of annoyance, isolation, unhappiness, and disappointment. Compromise is very necessary here.

You want to avoid the blame game at all costs. Here are some tips for doing that.

- **Find your reason.**

Think about why you're engaging in blaming your partner. Do you want to correct their behavior, or do you just want to vent and lash out at them? Discovering the intention behind your behavior can help you decide if you are in the wrong or not.

- **Accept that blaming each other is poor communication.**

Blaming your partner isn't an effective way of communicating with them because you are essentially accusing them of wrongdoing, putting them on the defensive. Why not try getting your message across with empathy, love, and compassion? These are ways that have been proven to affect the people around you positively and that can actually trigger a change.

Helping Each Other Through Bad Habits

Okay, let's face it, relationships can be rosy and lovey-dovey, but bad habits can quickly change all that. They might even be the source of conflicts in your relationship. Unfortunately, breaking a bad habit isn't easy, and quarreling with your spouse over a particularly bad habit can stress them out and drive them to continue that habit.

So what's the best way to help your partner break a bad habit? How can your partner support you to break yours? Bear in mind that you have to find a way to break this habit without resorting to further conflict in the relationship. It sounds like a tall order, but it's entirely possible.

The first step is to approach your partner in an empathetic manner and focus on the solution. Most times when we approach our significant other about their bad habit, we attack or confront them, not realizing that this is far from the best way to get a positive response. I mean, would you enjoy being attacked because of something you've been doing habitually? Of course not. It's better to discuss things with your partner in a soft, gentle manner.

Tell your partner exactly how you feel about their habit and show them you understand where they're coming from. Encourage them to drop the habit. Communicate your worry as clearly as possible. A good way to do this is to use statements that explain your reaction to the habit. For example, you can say something like, "When you smoke cigarettes, I get scared for our fertility as a couple." Tell them how relieved and happy you'd feel if they broke that habit.

Make sure to pick the right time to engage with your spouse. Approaching them about a bad habit when they're already in a bad mood might not be the best idea. Pick a time when your partner is relaxed and gently bring up the issue in a non-confrontational manner.

Offer positive reinforcement. Encourage your partner to break the habit by offering an incentive if they do. You must also be ready to hear about your own bad habits as well. This might be because they're feeling defensive about what you've told them. But don't get upset or accuse your partner of changing the subject. Both of you can agree to change your bad behavior and receive a joint reward when you're successful. This is a great way to improve communication and foster intimacy in a relationship.

I love talking about this topic in particular because it shows how teamwork can be used as an instrument to deepen the communication between your spouse and yourself.

Wrapping Up

I'm glad to see that you've made it this far. We've made a lot of progress, and by now, if you've been implementing what we've talked about, you should be seeing a huge difference in your relationship with your significant other, and perhaps even in your other relationships.

But, just like learning to ride a bike, sometimes you may fall off and it seems like the end of the world. Let me just say that it's very possible to slip back into old habits if you're not careful. Relapses are real. In the next chapter, we'll talk about what to do when this happens and how to get over it.

Your Quick Workbook

Has your relationship been emotionally draining, and how is this affecting your life as a whole?

_____

_____

_____

_____

_____

Do you think positivity is a possibility in your relationship?

_____

_____

_____

Have you ever considered your self-limiting thoughts as a reason for the constant negativity in your relationship?

Does your partner have bad habits that annoy you? Has your partner complained about any bad habits of yours? What move have you made towards breaking these bad habits?

PART 3

Preventing Relapses and Keeping Things Going

Identifying a problem and its solution is wonderful. It's commendable, in fact, and I'd like to let you know you're doing great. It's important, however, to keep your growth intact. Now that you have seen just how overthinking might be making your relationship difficult, it's time to look at how to harness the principle of taking it one day at a time and moving forward steadily with your partner. Let's dive in for the final swim.

CHAPTER 7

THE ART OF LISTENING, TRUSTING, AND LOVING FIERCELY LISTENING: MORE THAN JUST HEARING

When our marriage got to year 13, I felt like my wife stopped listening altogether. Every time I attempted to make conversation with her, she'd be too preoccupied with our financial problems and would not give coherent responses to what I said. This went on for two years, and I felt constantly unheard until I couldn't take it anymore. In a fit of anger, she threatened me with divorce, and I dared her. We both still regret everything we did after that. Our daughter hates us for ruining her life.

—Jason

Isn't it funny how some people seem to have excellent communication skills, yet they really don't? They *hmm* and *aah* at all the right places and always give off the vibe that they know just the right thing to say or the right gesture to make to keep you going. I mean, they stare at you directly, like they're gazing right into your soul, leaning forward and nodding, and you can't possibly doubt that they're listening to you.

If only that were completely true!

Communication skills are very important, as they help you connect better, but if you're not listening effectively, your communication is fundamentally flawed. The truth is, sometimes you're practicing these communication tips, unless you're a natural-born conversationalist, you might be so focused on *showing* someone that you're listening that you end up actually missing a large part of the conversation.

Listening is a skill nobody wants to admit they don't have. I mean, isn't it just hearing whatever someone is saying to you? All you need to do is concentrate and give them your full attention; how hard can that be, right?

Wrong.

Sorry to break it to you, friend, but listening and hearing are two different things, and you can be hearing what a person is saying without actually listening to them. It takes effort and focus to listen. And let's be honest here, although the Bible speaks about being quick to listen, slow to speak, and slow to anger, it's much easier to switch things up and be quick to speak and quick to anger, especially when you've been hurt by the person you're speaking with.

You're probably thinking, "Okay, so hearing is not listening and listening is not hearing. Fine, I get it. What's the difference between hearing and listening, then?"

Simply put, hearing is **passive** while listening is **active**. Hearing is the ability to perceive sound. You can't close your ears or ask them to stop functioning. The most you can do if you don't want to hear someone speaking is leave the room, or ask the person to stop talking if what they're saying is getting on your nerves, or you're in a bad mood and their voice is grating on your ears, or you're preoccupied and what they're saying just goes in one ear and out the other.

Listening, on the other hand, is voluntary. It's a choice you've made to concentrate and give your thoughtful attention to what the other person is saying. When listening for real, you're taking in the information a person is giving you and trying to understand what they're saying from their perspective.

Many times, before listening to their partner's perspective, an overthinker will have already made up their mind about the situation. Before your spouse gets the chance to speak about something, you've imagined different scenarios and drawn up your conclusion. You've made up your mind, and you're just giving your partner a chance to speak so that you can say, "Let it be known that I heard you out," or because it's the Christian thing to do. Well, making up your mind before listening to what your partner wants to say doesn't exactly make for a peaceful relationship, and if you've already decided something about a discussion that hasn't even been had, listening is going to prove difficult for you.

If you nag your partner sometimes for not listening to your needs and feelings, think about whether you're a good listener as well—because, let's face it, you can't expect your partner to listen to you if you won't listen to them.

If you're thinking, "Listening is too hard. I'm reading this book because I overthink a lot, and now you're asking me to set aside my assumptions and thoughts and listen without judgment?"—relax. I understand your concern, but it's possible to become an expert in listening, even if you're struggling with overthinking right now. After all, there are many instances in the Bible where Jesus showed superb listening skills, and hasn't He assured us that what He did, we can do even more?

How to Pay Attention to Your Partner's Nonverbal Communication

The success of any relationship can be said to rest almost solely on how well both parties fare at communication. One study found that 67.5% of marriages that end in divorce are due to communication problems (Boyd, 2022). I guess it's safe to say that communication is the foundation for any healthy relationship that plans to stand the test of time.

Verbal communication is always lauded as the most important aspect of communication, but nonverbal communication, while often overlooked, is just as crucial. If you want a successful marriage with the person you love, you need to master nonverbal communication in all its diverse forms. I'm always excited to talk about nonverbal communication because I love watching people's eyes light up when they realize how profound the effects of nonverbal communication can be. Let's jump right in!

Nonverbal communication, also known as manual communication, is basically speaking with every body part except your mouth. It involves gestures, body movement, and expressions like pulling back when hurt, walking off when annoyed, twirling hair when nervous, biting nails when anxious, and being short with someone when irritated or pissed. Nonverbal communication is the message that gets passed along without any trace of a sound. It could be a look, a nod, a disapproving curl of the lips, a smirk—it all counts.

Oftentimes, we can tell that our partner loves us through nonverbal communication. It's in the little things like preparing a warm bath for you after a long day, surprise gifts and dates, the way their face lights up when you walk into the room, or how they hug you from behind. Likewise, it's easy to know when your partner is upset based on their nonverbal cues—for instance, when they're not talking as much as usual, they give you the cold shoulder, or they go from chatty and bubbly to silent and withdrawn mid-conversation. Perhaps they have the habit of greeting you with a hug and a kiss when they get home at the end of the day, but they've recently stopped doing that, or they offer a halfhearted hug without the kiss. You don't need a therapist to tell you that something's changed.

There's a meme that jokes about what women really need when they say they want space and attention at the same time; it's a bit inane, but one thing we can't deny is the fact that we're complicated creatures, no matter our gender. Needless to say, learning to communicate properly with your partner will go a long way towards helping you unfold the mysteries of human nature.

It's likely that there have been times when you didn't realize your partner was broadcasting their emotions loud and clear without saying a word. You probably couldn't correctly decipher their body language, and of course, arguments won't be far off in situations like that.

Trust me, I know.

I know it can be quite frustrating because you most likely didn't even know they were angry in the first place, and suddenly they're fuming. And then perhaps they get even more upset after they realize that you never even noticed they were angry. Or—this is my favorite—they get annoyed because you didn't apologize for something that upset them that you didn't even *know* you did. I'll be real with you, it's enough to drive any well-meaning person up the wall.

So, what's the way forward?

Maybe it's learning how to listen effectively. Of course, being an effective listener is important for a healthy relationship, but it's not *just* about listening to whatever they say and examining their words over and over for hints of trouble before it starts. Nope. That's heading into overthinking territory, and the whole point here is to avoid that. Effective listening is about listening to what is said, and also what *isn't* said. Now, make no mistake, I'm not asking you to be some sort of mind reader or something weird like that. No need for that because, frankly speaking, it's just not possible.

But if you've been with your partner for a while now, being able to recognize some of their nonverbal tells should be your forte. You should be able to tell when their mouth is saying one thing and their body language is saying something else entirely. If you can, that's great! If you can't, sit tight because I'm about to show you stuff.

Let's take a look at various types of nonverbal communication, shall we?

1. Facial expressions

Some of us have very expressive faces, like me. My wife can immediately tell how I feel about something just by looking at my face when she brings it up. I believe facial expressions are the easiest form of nonverbal communication to understand. Your facial expressions can communicate happiness, sadness, anger, disgust, surprise, and fear. Those emotions are pretty much the same everywhere. If your partner is claiming to be happy and is frowning, it's easy to identify that their words and facial expression don't match. As far as I know, frowning signifies anger or displeasure and a smirk could mean mockery. I'll go out on a limb here and assume it's the same for you too.

Anyway, for people with faces that are hard to read, two solutions come to mind. The first is microexpressions. Microexpressions are facial expressions that are very brief in duration, lasting less than one second (Svetevia, 2016). Research suggests that everyone has microexpressions, no matter who they are, and most microexpressions look the same on different faces. It's fascinating and very useful in behavioral analysis.

The second solution is to look for other nonverbal indicators. Is their face not giving you any clues? Check the rest of their body language. Keep reading to learn more about the other types of body language.

2. Movement and posture

This includes how you sit, stand, and walk, as well as your stance, bearing, and how you basically carry yourself. Did you know you can identify whether someone has feelings for you based on their posture? For example, when they're leaning towards you, or their feet are facing in your direction, it could mean that person has a little crush on you. You can guess that your partner is tense if they're pacing nervously, or if their body is stiff, or their shoulders are squared.

3. Gestures

We use gestures a lot, especially when we're speaking animatedly about something that interests us. Gestures are mostly involuntary. They include things like pointing, beckoning, waving, and running your fingers through your hair.

4. Eye contact

It's important to maintain eye contact to keep the flow of a conversation. You can gauge a listener's interest or lack thereof by how well they make eye contact as you talk. If they have shifty eyes or find it difficult to maintain eye contact, it could mean they're hiding something or lying.

5. Touch

Now, this is an important part of relationships. How your partner feels can be easily communicated through touch. A pat on the back, holding hands, or putting an arm around the other person can be used to convey love and affection. A firm handshake can sometimes be used to assert control. A fist bump is a clear sign of friendship.

6. Space

Depending on your relationship or how you feel about someone in a given moment, it may seem like someone is invading your personal space if they stand too close. Other times, you may feel like they're not close enough. You may be able to guess that your partner is in a sour mood or has something on their mind when they don't want you in their space.

7. Voice

Sometimes, our feelings and emotions can be so overwhelming that they seep out and are evident in our voices. The tone of your voice can sometimes indicate hurt, sarcasm, anger, or even confidence. Paying attention to things like how loud your partner is speaking, their tone, and their inflection will give you valuable information about how your partner feels.

Now that we've covered the different types of nonverbal communication, let's discuss how to observe and identify these signals so you can better understand your partner's feelings, moods, and actions. This will definitely help you to improve your connection with your partner.

Here are some tips to help you decode body language easily:

- **Watch out for inconsistencies.**

These discrepancies may seem insignificant, but they're actually quite important. If your partner is saying something but their body language is saying something else, you might want to look closely into that situation because something doesn't add up. A nonverbal cue should support what the person is saying, not negate it.

- **Take note of all the nonverbal signals.**

While each nonverbal cue could signal one thing or another, a combination of these nonverbal cues can mean something else as a whole. Consider eye contact, tone of voice, posture, and body movement—when taken together, are these signals consistent with what they're saying?

With these tips, evaluating nonverbal cues should become very easy.

So, what should you look for when you're assessing each type of body language?

1. Facial expressions

Check whether the person's facial expression appears mask-like and uninterested, or if their face is expressive and indicates that they're interested in what you have to say. They could also slightly lift their eyebrows to show surprise, discomfort, or skepticism based on the context. The eyebrow lift can also come with a smile, which may indicate that they find what you're saying interesting or are just playing with you.

2. Posture and gesture

Is their body stiff or relaxed and comfortable? Do they keep checking the time or constantly change their posture, showing impatience? They might fidget, which can indicate boredom, anxiety, or irritation. Do their shoulders appear raised, tense, or relaxed? Are their fists clenched and their arms crossed while you're asking them about something? That might mean they're getting defensive.

3. Eye contact

Are they making eye contact or not? And if they are, does it feel natural, or does it seem overly intense?

4. Touch

You should note the presence or absence of physical touch. Sometimes it might not be absent, just reduced. The way they touch you also matters—does it scream possessiveness or just tenderness and care? Is their grip on you a little too tight?

5. Tone and voice

Does their tone sound flat and uninterested? Animated? Or is it sounding a little over the top or like they're forcing it?

6. Timing and place

Timing and place really matter, and nonverbal cues can give you clues as to whether it's the right time and place for a conversation or not. Your partner could slightly shake their head to indicate "not now" or tilt their head to the side as if saying, "Let's go there." Even if they don't give these signs, you can confirm whether or not there's a back-and-forth rapport, or the rate at which your partner gives their nonverbal responses.

That's basically it. However, keep in mind that it's not uncommon to misunderstand nonverbal cues, in which case you can simply ask your partner what they're feeling. Nevertheless, understanding nonverbal cues will help your relationship a lot. Since you can tell a lot about how they're feeling at that moment, you can more easily avoid arguments or uncomfortable situations, settle issues amicably, and figure out the root of the problem when something isn't right.

Using Nonviolent Communication to Improve Your Relationship/Marriage

Listening to and understanding body language helps to enhance effective communication between you and your partner. Clearly, communication is a two-way street. The Bible says wives should be submissive and husbands should love their wives as themselves (Ephesians 5:22, 23). But that can be difficult to do, and gets pretty frustrating when it seems like you're the only one seeing the problem and trying to work on the relationship. We're only human, after all, and sometimes we need a little effort from our partner to show they care. That's why both spouses must work on this together.

Did you know that when you change your mode of communication, you're automatically influencing your relationship with your partner? The important thing here is deciding to change your mode of communication for the better. One great tool I frequently recommend is nonviolent communication (NVC), a set of principles developed in the 1960s by psychologist Marshall Rosenberg. This tool has helped a lot of couples take their communication game to the next level.

Your approach to communication in romantic relationships should be a reflection of the old proverb, "Dig your well before you're thirsty." Thirst here is a metaphor for your need to connect, and for the mutual understanding and trust that is essential for your partnership. Digging the well involves practicing nonviolent communication and becoming skillful at it so that you'll have those tools ready when you need them.

Most people are skeptical about the NVC approach at first; some have accused it of feeling unnatural and scripted. But after they practice it for a while, they frequently have no choice but to admit that it makes a notable difference. They can't seem to stop raving about how much their communication with their partner has improved as well as how their connection to each other has been reinforced.

The mistake most couples make is that they wait till there's a full-blown conflict before they decide to work on their communication skills. Don't wait till you get to that point. Even if you're already in a full-blown conflict, don't worry, the NVC tool can turn things around.

Usually, the way NVC works is that when we find ourselves in distressing situations or situations of conflict, we must take time to think before making our grievances known to our partner.

So, instead of saying, "Derek, you're always leaving your stuff lying around and expecting me to pick up after you like a maid. That's really disgusting. I'm not picking up after you today; clean up your mess yourself!"—NVC instructs you to stop, think, and rephrase that statement. I mean, you don't actually expect Derek to respond well to that, do you? NVC acknowledges that our automatic responses to situations will usually hurt the people we love. It focuses on being more compassionate and empathetic when communicating your feelings.

NVC sounds so simple that you're probably thinking, "Okay, so I just have to think before I speak, right?"

I don't mean to burst your bubble, but it's not that easy. Especially if the reason you want to improve your communication skills is to get your partner to always agree with you. NVC is not a manipulation tool; rather, the key components of this tool are purpose, attention, and intention. The goal of using this strategy is to connect on a deeper level so that contributing to each other's well-being will come easily to you and your partner. It aims to create win-win situations, not an I-must-always-win situation.

I know, I know, I've gone on and on about NVC and how important it is for effective communication and a deeper connection with your partner—but it's just so awesome, I can't help it. All right, let's dive right into the four steps of nonviolent communication.

1. Observe the facts

Most times when we experience distressing situations, like Derek leaving his stuff lying around despite the number of times his partner has spoken to him about it, it's hard to look at the situation objectively. This step entails focusing on the facts without being judgmental, and avoiding the use of words like "always," "often," and "never."

When you stick to the facts, it's easier to connect with the other person without them having to be on the defensive, whereas when you talk about your interpretation or judge the situation, the other person is more likely to hear blame and criticism, and they put their guard up almost immediately. Let's look at these examples:

Observation: "You promised to take the trash out two days ago, and I had to take it out myself just this morning."

Interpretation/judgment: "You're unreliable and never helpful around the house, and even the one thing I asked you to help me with, I ended up doing myself."

2. Note feelings

This second step involves describing the emotions these situations make you feel. Our interpretations and judgments of situations are often a result of our feelings being expressed as thoughts or observations. So, when describing your feelings, don't do it as a mash-up of your interpretation of someone else's actions and your thoughts; instead, share only the emotions you experience.

For instance:

Feelings: "I am excited," "I feel irritated," "I feel frustrated."

Interpretation and thoughts: "You don't care about me. You think I'm worthless."

3. Uncover desires

NVC focuses on needs—after all, most of the emotions we feel center on whether our needs are being met or not. We tend to blame the person or situation that made us feel a certain way. Instead of blaming others for the way you feel, you can find other strategies to satisfy that unmet need. Fortunately, one strategy can satisfy many needs, and a particular need can at times be satisfied by a million different strategies.

Let's look at an example of what I mean by that.

Need: Authenticity

Strategies for meeting this need: Telling your partner what you don't like instead of bottling up your emotions, doing things you feel passionate about, and excusing yourself from uncomfortable situations.

4. Make requests

This final step is about expressing your request clearly and concisely. My wife was telling me how women especially may tend to keep quiet or give vague requests, expecting that their partner will find out what they want them to do on their own. She used to do this to me a lot back when we were younger. However, doing this is setting yourself up for disappointment, as most times, it results in your needs not being fulfilled.

You should also know that making a request is different from demanding something. Asking your spouse to please put the dishes in the dishwasher and saying, "You'd better put your plate in the dishwasher" are two very different things. Also, your request should be doable and clearly state what you want or don't want.

Now, let's combine the four steps to restructure the statement made to Derek earlier:

"Derek, I found your stuff thrown all around the room when I got back from work today, and it made me feel irritated and annoyed. I know that's not your intention; it probably just got to me because I like things to be organized and I had a stressful day at work. Do you think you could pick everything up and put it away instead, please?"

How does that sound? Better, right? You can probably see how using these steps will make communication a lot easier and smoother, and also help you avoid conflict in your relationship.

How to Love Fiercely Despite the Tendency to Overthink

Yes, it's normal to overthink things, and it shouldn't be surprising to find that romantic partnerships, too, are often the subject of a lot of overthinking. However, by this point in the book, you have likely realized that if you're not careful, overthinking could sabotage your relationship. As an overthinker, you might start inventing nonexistent issues about the relationship, which can make you miserable and affect your mental health.

We've already established the common reasons why you might be overthinking your relationship; now the big question is: Is it possible to still love your partner fiercely despite being an overthinker?

Learning to truly listen to what is said and what goes unsaid and practicing nonviolent communication are excellent ways to keep the flame of love burning despite your overthinking tendencies. Letting your partner know what you're feeling and thinking instead of constantly second-guessing yourself or repressing your feelings is important as well. Also, be sure to ask your spouse what they mean when they say or do something that you're not sure how to interpret—or you can simply tell them if they've said or done something that makes you feel uncomfortable.

Since you've acknowledged the fact that you overthink everything, a simple solution to handle these thoughts that pop into your mind is cognitive restructuring. This process turns negative automatic thoughts into positive ones. Cognitive restructuring works by finding evidence to support your assumptions. If you don't find any, it's easier to let go of these thoughts.

A key secret to loving your partner despite your tendency to overthink is trusting them. I know that trust doesn't come easy, especially for overthinkers, that's for sure. But unless your partner has proven untrustworthy, I believe you should give trusting them a go. This is so important because trust lays the foundation for a healthy, happy relationship.

I remember a young woman named Jolene who had a tendency to overthink things. If you merely looked at her the wrong way, *bam*! She'd go off assuming the worst. That was before she got married to Dave. He is one of the sweetest, most caring men I know, and fortunately, he's very compassionate and quite empathetic toward Jolene's overthinking tendencies. But Jolene's previous relationship was with a chronic cheater, sadly. Thus, she didn't trust Dave one bit when they began dating. She was always going through his phone, picking fights if he so much as glanced at another woman, overthinking all his nice gestures—it practically ruined the relationship.

I had to sit her down one day and tell her to open up her heart to trusting Dave, and she admitted that he had never given her a reason to doubt his faithfulness. She really tried—God bless her heart, she did. It took a while, and they're a work in progress, but their relationship is a loving, happy one now, and I couldn't be happier for them.

How to Build Trust in Your Relationship

1. Be honest, accept your emotions, and practice vulnerability

Ask your partner for assurance if you need it. Tell them if you're feeling uneasy. Invite them to get to know you, how you feel about their words or actions, and how you want them to feel. Be honest about your dreams, worries, and aspirations.

2. Assume your partner's intentions are good

If your spouse lets you down, remember that it might not have been on purpose; mistakes can happen. While it's acceptable to speculate about their motivations, remain open to the possibility that they may have made a simple error. Forgive them. Don't forget what the Bible says about forgiveness—forbearing one another and forgiving one another: "If any man has a quarrel against any, even as Christ forgave you, so also do ye" (Colossians 3:13).

3. Talk openly and honestly about important issues

Spend some time each day checking in, facing one another, and considering how things are going. If there are problems in your relationship, address them right away rather than letting them fester. Start off simple, use sentences that start with "I" ("I feel," "I notice," "I wonder"), and be honest. The Bible says not to let the sun set on your anger, but I think you should apply that verse to any issues troubling your relationship, too. Say it and get it off your chest; you'll definitely sleep better that way.

4. Recognize how previous wrongs can lead to mistrust

Consider whether your lack of trust is a result of your partner's behavior, your own fears, or both. Be mindful of any unsolved problems or trauma from previous relationships that might be causing mistrust right now.

5. Practice mending fences after a dispute

If you're feeling overwhelmed during a discussion or argument with your partner, take a quick pause to consider what just transpired. This will give you both some time to cool off and gather your thoughts so you can talk to each other in a more meaningful and productive way.

6. Be aware that stating your needs is not being needy

When our partners fail to satisfy our needs, we tend to become incredibly irate and dissatisfied. But have you stopped to consider whether you've clearly articulated this need to your spouse? Have you given them instructions on how to meet it? Most of the time, our partners can't read our minds; therefore, we have to teach them how to meet our needs and help us feel loved.

So that's it! As long as there's mutual trust in your relationship, it is completely possible to love your partner fiercely despite being an overthinker. Choose to trust your partner today. You'll be glad you did.

Wrapping Up

When I discovered just how critical body language is for communication, and what an important tool it can be, it opened up a whole new world of communication for me. The ability of you and your significant other to understand each other's needs and respond to them appropriately brings a new dimension of contentment and happiness to the relationship.

This could be you too. We've learned a lot so far, and I'd like to say that your relationship is worth it. Your happiness is worth it. Your joy is worth it. Keep applying what you've learned, and keep pressing for more. The rewards are unquantifiable.

At this point, maybe you've been wondering: "Okay, so let's say I follow all these steps, improve my relationship with my partner, and reduce my tendency to overthink—but what if I slip back into overthinking when I start feeling anxious again? Is it possible to actually prevent overthinking relapses? Can I stop them from occurring?" I'd turn to the next (and final) chapter to find out. See you there!

Your Quick Workbook

Do your overthinking tendencies tend to get in the way of your ability to listen effectively without being judgmental or doubtful?

_____

_____

_____

_____

_____

Do you and your partner use nonverbal communication a lot? How well do you recognize each other's cues?

_____

_____

_____

_____

_____

_____

What do you think about nonviolent communication (NVC) techniques? Is NVC something you're open to trying out?

_____

_____

_____

_____

_____

CHAPTER 8

PREVENTING OVERTHINKING RELAPSES TO PREVENT CONFLICT AND TRUST ISSUES

"In the multitude of my thoughts within me, Thy comfort delights my soul."

—Psalm 94:19

Anticipating Overthinking Triggers

If overthinking is a long-term habit, you obviously can't just put a lid on it and say adios just like that. Habits can be very hard to break, and it's natural to expect that your overthinking tendencies won't go away instantly.

Overthinking can be triggered by a lot of factors. Let's consider six triggers/possible causes of your overthinking habit:

1. Anxiety disorders

If you've already been diagnosed with an anxiety disorder, you probably know that overthinking is a classic symptom. Anxiety causes you to automatically overthink everything and assume the worst of most things. Keep in mind that although it is tough for a person with an anxiety disorder to get over their overthinking tendencies, it's not impossible.

2. Regrets

Sometimes it's hard to let go of past mistakes, which can be problematic. It's good to reminisce on the past from time to time, especially to relive good memories, but sometimes we tend to stress over mistakes made in the past and wonder how we could have prevented them.

This line of thinking is impractical and a waste of energy. No matter what we do now, we can't undo the past; we can only learn from our mistakes and become better people. Make peace with your past, and if you're still struggling to let go, you can do something that serves as a quick fix. For instance, if you were really unkind to someone in the past, you can try asking for their forgiveness.

3. Childhood trauma

We all know that our childhood experiences can leave a lasting impact on us. Well, overthinking is one of the aftermaths of having a terrible childhood. Kids tend to withdraw into themselves and overthink as coping mechanisms to get them through tough and scary situations. The unfortunate part is that this tendency becomes a habit and persists right through to adulthood. Reframing and resetting these habits might be difficult for an adult, especially one whose mind has been set to naturally overthink things, but it is doable (thank God for that).

4. A need to always be in control

Some people want to be in control of everything. Maybe you want things to go exactly the way you'd prefer, and you believe the only way to pull that off is to try to control everything. That makes a lot of sense; I can't deny that.

Taking control of situations and people has its clear advantages, but it has its cons too. Apart from being an indicator that you lack confidence in other people's skills, which could affect your personal and professional relationships, it also frequently leads to overthinking. Since you want everything to be perfect, you end up stressing about every detail, and whether you got something wrong or not. If you're this kind of person, start letting go gradually. Doing it all at once would be difficult, but start gradually delegating tasks to others. This improves your interpersonal relationships and reduces your overthinking and stress.

5. Personal worries

We all worry about things—our job, health, money, relationships. But believe me, there's a reason why the Lord asks us to cast all our burdens on Him. Worrying too much affects your mental, physical, and spiritual health. And does worrying solve anything? Absolutely not. Instead, you can make a list of the things you're worrying about, set a time to do something about them, and enumerate the steps you can take to solve each problem. Worrying will not solve anything, says the Bible: *"...and which of you with taking thoughts can add to his stature one cubit?"* (Matthew 6:27)

6. Uncertainty

Not knowing what to expect of the future can be scary sometimes. Some people worry about the future more than average—about whether they'll fulfill their dream of working a job they're passionate about, whether they'll have a disabled kid, when their parents might die, and the list goes on and on. But overthinking the future is not helping anyone, especially not you; you'll only end up inventing scenarios in your head for questions you don't have the answer to.

Rather than stress about the uncertain future, why not talk to God about it? After all, He knows the end from the beginning. If your automatic response to new, uncertain situations is panic, it's important to reframe your mindset. The future is unknown to us, so just live every day as if it's your last and stop stressing about the future.

Remember, your overthinking triggers are unique to you. We've all had different life experiences and handle distressing situations differently. Even if you can't relate to any of the reasons listed above, take time to reflect on your unique experiences that may be affecting your tendency to overthink.

If you pay attention to your overthinking patterns, I'm sure you'll notice that you tend to overthink due to specific situations. It may be when you're feeling sad, stressed out, sleep-deprived, or alone. Paying attention to your triggers is one way of preventing your overthinking relapses. So, observe the situations when you catch yourself overthinking and pick out the common triggers during these instances.

Prioritizing Sharing About Each Other's Day

I know I've reiterated this point again and again, but the importance of communication in a healthy relationship cannot be overemphasized. Between going to work, taking care of the kids, cooking, and all the other things that take up our time, communicating with your spouse can be overwhelming. Time flies, and before you know it, you can barely find a spare minute to have meaningful, deep conversations. Suddenly, neither person is making an effort anymore because you're both engrossed in your day-to-day activities. It becomes easy to start thinking that your partner prefers work or playing with the kids to spending time with you. Throw in a few incidents of coming home late and your overthinking brain goes into overdrive and pushes your relationship downhill.

I can hear you asking, "So how do I avoid this? My partner and I are so busy, and it's hard to find time."

The truth is, you have to *make* the time, and you have to prioritize your marriage. If you can't find time to talk because you or your partner spend the whole evening taking care of the kids and you get so tired that you just go to bed immediately, you're not doing something right. Have you ever thought about what goes on in the minds of kids whose parents split up? If your relationship is not solid, there's no teamwork, and it's possible that your kids won't have a family unit anymore if things deteriorate.

So, how do you prioritize your relationship? Spend quality time together.

Talk about your day. Have a bit of alone time together. A great trick for people with busy days is to schedule it right into your day and stick to that schedule. You and your partner should commit to this. It could be something as small as going to bed together a few minutes earlier than usual or planning date nights. Ladies, let your little black dress see the light of day once more. I'm sure when your love was still young and budding, you enjoyed talking about your day with your partner after being apart. It's high time you reignited that spark.

Instead of overthinking how rude your colleague was to you, go on and rant about everything to your partner; after all, they're supposed to be your confidante.

Making Positivity a Daily Habit in Your Home

Several relationship experts continuously emphasize the importance of positivity in our relationships. If you've ever listened to or read something by Pat Love, John Gottman, and many others, then you'll have noticed how they're constantly stressing this fact. And it's true: the adverse effect of negative energy on relationships doesn't need much explanation.

But let's be honest here, being positive all the time is hard. It's like there's always negative energy around. Disappointments, stress from your job, life issues, and the like can make maintaining positivity difficult. We're more inclined to negative thoughts because our brains have been wired for survival. Considering the worst possible scenarios may just be our way of protecting ourselves.

But positivity means a happy, long-lasting relationship, so how do we go about achieving it?

Becoming more positive isn't just about deciding to think positive thoughts. Most of us are inclined to see the negative side of things, so there's a need to reframe your mind and address issues that may be the cause of your negativity.

Here's how to make positivity a daily habit in your home:

1. Take a break from all forms of negativity

I learned this from Harville Hendrix (author of *Getting the Love You Want*, among other books), put it into practice, and trust me, it worked. So how does this work? You and your partner should avoid criticizing, shifting blame, or expressing any shame. No matter how tempting it might be, you have to persevere on this. In fact, during this period you might notice their annoying personality quirks and feel like saying something just a teensy bit critical—but you have to hold back. It can be quite maddening, I know, but don't give up and you'll see the benefits. Another great tip is to focus on things you love about your partner instead of dwelling on the negatives.

2. Compliment and appreciate your partner

Tell your spouse what you appreciate about them. This encourages you to focus on the positive rather than the negative. Saying things like, "I love how you look in that dress," "I appreciate your driving me to and from work because my car acted up," or "I appreciate your sense of humor" are simple ways to start.

3. Reminisce about happy memories

Everyone is always talking about the honeymoon phase in relationships. I doubt there's any relationship that hasn't gone through this phase. You might be wondering how you went from that phase to the current, not-so-lovey-dovey phase you're in, but that's what happens if you're not intentional about the relationship. Looking back at those happy times is great, but don't stop there. Try to recreate those awesome memories; you'll be glad you did.

4. Be realistic

No relationship is perfect, that much is clear. You might not have noticed some flaws in the honeymoon phase, but when that wears off, you'll have to deal with the realities of a long-term committed relationship. Also, you know who you married, and you can't expect your partner to make unrealistic changes.

5. Make clear requests

Your partner is not a mind reader; if you want something or have an issue with how they dealt with something, let them know. Good communication automatically makes a relationship better. And don't forget to practice NVC when doing this—remember, the way you deliver your message matters a lot.

6. Take ownership of your part in a conflict

You shouldn't always assume, or allow your partner to assume, all the responsibility for a conflict. Own your role in it and share what you learned about yourself in the course of the argument. For instance: "I realized during our argument that I was too harsh in trying to correct you; next time I would like to take a softer approach."

7. Create positive responses to negative thoughts

As I mentioned earlier, external stressors are bound to bring about negativity. Try replacing every negative thought with a positive one. After all, you need positive energy if you're going to be practicing positivity.

My partner and I use some of these practices in our relationship. We're not a perfect couple (we're a work in progress), but these practices are doing wonders for our marriage. As you know, a happy relationship means we're also happy in our daily lives. We've made it a habit to appreciate each other constantly and to communicate our issues clearly and gently avoid conflicts. We're also always on the lookout for negativity, and when it arises, we deal with it as a couple.

Practicing all these steps at once may not be practical for you, though, since you're just starting out. Take it one step at a time. Start from those that seem the easiest to you and gradually integrate more of them into your home. Make them a part of your partnership and you'll fall in love with the process, and with your spouse, more and more.

How to Efficiently Prevent Relapses with Your Overthinking

Picture this: You've been waking up at 6:00 a.m. every morning for the past five years, and the first thing you do is drink coffee. You know you're not fully awake without caffeine in your system. Then, you put on your running gear, go for a run, get back home, take a shower, eat breakfast, and hurry to work. One day, after five years of this routine, you decide to take a break from coffee because you read an article that spoke about the dangers of excessive caffeine intake. I can bet your first day would be hellish. You'd probably have a headache, feel irritable and tired, and be tempted to take just one sip of coffee. But you make it through nine caffeine-free days (and you swear that those days are the hardest), and now you're confident that you can function perfectly without caffeine. Then one morning, weeks later, after you're sure you've conquered the need for caffeine, you wake up with an unexpected, serious craving for coffee—what do you do?

Humans are creatures of habit, and habits die hard, that's for sure. You've been overthinking for so long, and now you're making an effort to stop; does that mean you'll never feel the urge to overthink a situation again? That's doubtful.

Since you've identified your overthinking triggers, when you experience them, you can easily prevent a relapse based on these tips:

1. Find a distraction

Engage in something you enjoy to stop yourself from overthinking. I'm sure you have a lot of hobbies or activities that interest you and will keep your mind off these negative thoughts for a while. It could be creative, like attempting a new recipe or picking up some new cooking techniques, or you might have to work it out by going to your preferred exercise class. You could also try to acquire a new interest, like painting or pottery, or do volunteer work with a neighborhood organization to make a change. By the time you're done, you'll probably have forgotten what you were thinking about.

You should put some of these activities in your schedule; they'll help you reduce your anxiety level and stop focusing on negativity.

2. Get help from friends, loved ones, or your partner

If you keep overthinking a situation or occurrence, you can ask your friends or partner to weigh in on the matter. They may give you a fresh perspective or help you find a solution to the issue so that you won't have to continue stressing about it.

3. Challenge your thoughts

You don't have to believe your thoughts 100%. After viewing them objectively, you might realize that the thought is baseless. Find out if there's any evidence in support of or against the thought. That way, you can easily determine if it's logical or helpful. It's easy to squash your overthinking when you realize that what you're thinking is not supported by any facts. Then consider an alternative possibility for a broader, more balanced perspective on the situation.

4. Practice self-compassion

Being compassionate towards your friends or your partner probably comes easy to you. What about towards yourself, though? How does your internal monologue sound when you're dealing with an issue or challenge?

What does practicing self-compassion mean? It's about being able to show oneself love, kindness, and forgiveness. You will truly calm your body's internal threat system by doing that, which will give you a clearer head to address any issues.

5. Find comfort in God's Word

The Bible says, "In the multitude of my thoughts within me, thy comfort delights my soul" (Psalm 94:19). Often, it's only in God's Word that we can find true comfort. God's Word will bring you peace and put an end to your ruminating thoughts.

Communication Exercises to Strengthen Your Relationship with Your Partner

Talking, listening, being open, and understanding each other make for effective communication. Trust, love, and communication are the foundation of a successful relationship, which is why communication exercises are necessary tools for couples who want to improve their partnership.

One thing about these exercises, though: you must be willing to actually do them, and also get your partner on board. It's understandable that you and your partner barely have time for any extra activities with your busy schedule, so I won't waste your time with exercises that might not work. These exercises have been proven effective over and over again and have helped many people to greatly improve their relationships. In fact, a lot of couples have printed copies of these exercises to share the good news with those who might be in need of it.

Try each of these exercises out one by one, and choose the one that works best for you to continue implementing in your relationship.

1. Taking turns

Have you ever witnessed conversations where one person doesn't allow the other to complete what they're saying before speaking? This frequently happens in group conversations among friends, but it can happen between spouses as well. This exercise addresses that, giving both partners the opportunity to speak and be listened to.

Decide who will speak first and set a timer for three to five minutes. When the timer starts, one person begins speaking without interruption from the other. The other partner is not allowed to speak during this time, but they may express acknowledgment, understanding, and empathy through nonverbal cues.

Once the first person has completed speaking, the second asks questions to clarify what they have just heard (for example, "How did you feel when you told me that?" or "What can I do next time to make things better?" or even "Why is this so important to you?"). After these queries have been addressed and clarified, it is the other spouse's turn to speak without interruption.

This exercise teaches the pair of you to wait patiently for your turn and to respect each other's time and viewpoints.

2. Mirroring

When you mirror your spouse, you pay attention to his or her ideas and emotions before repeating what was said back to them and asking, "Did I get that right?" You can keep asking questions until your partner feels like they've been sufficiently heard, at which point they can either affirm or deny that you got it right. The listener might then support their partner by stating something like, "That makes sense" or "I'm glad you clarified that for me." Even if you don't quite agree with what was stated, at least now that you've heard them out, you can approach the argument with more understanding.

3. The "I" statement

One of the most well-known communication exercises for couples is the "I" statement technique. Here, you want to avoid accusing, blaming, criticizing, and shaming one another—all of which are frequent tactics couples use when they're at odds with one another. The issue with blaming and shaming is that rather than enhancing the relationship, it might cause distance or detachment.

Using "I" statements when you're angry or upset about something might help you take ownership of your emotions while lessening the amount of blame you place on your partner. In fact, studies have demonstrated that using the pronoun "I" rather than "you" lessens the possibility that conversations about conflict may result in a violent encounter. Finally, using "I" statements can enable us to forge stronger bonds with all the people in our lives, not only our romantic partners (Shane et al., 2022).

4. The 40-20-40 method

A specific communication exercise for compassionate listening and helpful conflict resolution is the 40-20-40 method. With this technique, the conversation's focus is divided into two parts: each person's feelings receive 40% of the attention, with 20% left over to talk about the relationship.

The aim is for each person to listen with the intention of understanding the other rather than defending themselves. Each person uses their allotted time to speak about their own feelings. In order to avoid seeming accusatory, it's best to only discuss how each person is feeling. The objective here is to show kindness and empathy to one another.

5. Fireside conversation

The term "fireside" connotes warmth, openness, and a say-anything attitude. President Franklin D. Roosevelt hosted what he called "fireside chats" over the radio to engage with the American people during World War II, bringing to mind the image of a friendly discussion with the president in front of a crackling fire. With this in mind, pick a place where you and your spouse feel at ease, order or prepare something yummy for both of you, and sit down together for a cozy conversation.

In order to give each other your entire attention during these conversations and to feel free to express whatever is on your mind, it is crucial that you remove all outside distractions.

You'll notice that these exercises cover verbal, nonverbal, and listening skills. They will help you and your partner learn more about each other and also help you clear the emotions, issues, and misunderstandings you've been piling up over time. Try to schedule one of these exercises as frequently as possible (at least once a week), and in no time, your relationship will improve due to effective communication.

Wrapping Up

Some of the strategies in this chapter might be common knowledge, but you've almost certainly learned one or two new things. While I'm sure that following the guidelines set out here will help a lot, it's entirely understandable if you get overwhelmed.

Especially if you're reading this for the first time and trying to get your head around everything in the book all at once.

Here's my advice: take it slow and use the workbook sections. You can come back to these tips as many times as you want. Remember that it's not a sprint, but a marathon.

Your Quick Workbook

How do you feel when, despite all your hard work, you relapse (or almost relapse) into your overthinking habits?

_____

_____

_____

_____

_____

Do you think spending quality time with your partner regularly is a habit you can make stick? Why or why not?

_____

_____

_____

_____

_____

Practicing positivity despite all the negativity around you might prove difficult; how are you feeling about it?

_____

_____

_____

_____

_____

What methods or strategies have you practiced in the past to help you handle your overthinking tendencies? Were they helpful?

_____

_____

_____

_____

_____

_____

Conclusion

Getting lost in your own negative, anxious thoughts can be damaging; it's like you're being sucked into a vortex, and you can't see or hear clearly, which makes you unable to view things objectively. You already have your own definitive thoughts about a situation, so whatever anyone else says doesn't make much sense to you.

Being trapped in a black hole of your own thoughts can be overwhelming. It gets even more terrifying when you realize that the vortex can show up at any time and swallow you up, stealing your time, happiness, and peace—and worst of all, holding you back from having a deeper connection with your partner.

How would you feel if all of that negativity and anxiety completely disappeared from your life? Or if you were able to prevent yourself from being sucked in in the first place? Freeing, right? Yep, freedom, love, laughter, and deeper connection are the keys to a happy life. And do you know the best part? You really can leave all your negativity behind you for good. It might be a lot of work, but the positivity you'll enjoy afterwards makes it totally worth it. You'll be able to enjoy the happiness and deep connection that comes with being in a healthy, long-lasting, committed relationship, maybe even enjoy that long-forgotten honeymoon phase again, and a lot of other couples around you will probably wonder how you and your partner are thriving.

That's the value you're getting from this book—the ability to let go of overthinking and all negativity and connect more deeply with your partner. And you know what the best part is? You can read this book over and over again to gain more insights; after all, it's yours.

Now that you know that your overthinking tendencies and anxiety are what have been putting a damper on your relationship and preventing you from communicating effectively with your partner, all that's left to do is utilize the tools packed in this book for a better, stronger, long-lasting relationship. Being fiercely in love is not only for those who have just fallen in love. You can also experience this, even if you've been with your spouse for decades.

Putting an end to your overthinking habits, managing your anxiety, and learning how to be a better communicator is important because once you tame the negativity and start practicing effective communication, it will propel your partner to make an effort too.

You should know that the journey won't be simple, though. Changing a long-term habit is no walk in the park. But as long as you can recognize your triggers and stop the thoughts before you enter another negative thought spiral, you're good to go.

The first step is becoming aware of your overthinking, which you have successfully done.

The next step involves dealing with all the negativity—your overthinking spirals, negative thoughts, negative energy, and conflict with your partner—which you can do using the tools we've discussed in this book. Then you can begin learning and practicing the art of effective communication and how to avoid relapsing. Acknowledging your issues, removing every trace of negativity from your thoughts, and preventing relapse might seem like a tall order, but don't give up. Having a happy relationship and life is definitely worth all the stress.

Remaining positive despite all the external stressors around you is going to prove challenging. Everything going on in the world right now is enough to put anyone in a sour mood for days. But the fact that you've made it to the end of the book shows how determined you are to improve your relationship. I know that managing to stay positive in this negative world is something you can do as well.

This book is the perfect guide to help you communicate and connect with your partner. Now that you have all the tools you need, go out there and use them. You're just a few steps away from enjoying the best years of your relationship.

If you got value from this book and enjoyed reading it, please leave a review on Amazon so other amazing people can have access to the tools in this book and improve their relationships as well. Gracias, amigo.

Thank You

Thank you so much for purchasing my book.

You could have picked from dozens of other books, but you took a chance and chose this one.

So, THANK YOU SO MUCH for getting this book and for making it all the way to the end.

Before you go, I wanted to ask you for one small favor. **Could you please consider writing a review on the platform? Posting a review is the best and easiest way to spread the word about this book and support healthy relationships in the lives of many couples.**

Let's do this together! Your review will help other people discover the information in this book, and your feedback will help me to keep writing the kinds of books that will help you get the results you want. I would love to hear from you.

>> Leave a review on Amazon US <<

https://www.amazon.com/review/create-review?&asin=XXXXXXX

>> Leave a review on Amazon UK <<

https://www.amazon.co.uk/review/create-review?&asin=XXXXXXX

Bonus

13 SCRIPTURES TO FIND COMFORT IN WHEN OVERTHINKING

1. 2 Corinthians 10:5: "We destroy every proud obstacle that keeps people from knowing God. We capture their rebellious thoughts and teach them to obey Christ."

2. Proverbs 12:25: "Anxiety weighs down the heart, but a kind word cheers it up."

3. Romans 12:2: "Don't copy the behavior and customs of this world, but let God transform you into a new person by changing the way you think. Then you will learn to know God's will for you, which is good and pleasing and perfect."

4. Isaiah 35:4: "Say to those with fearful hearts, 'Be strong, do not fear; your God will come, he will come with a vengeance; with divine retribution, he will come to save you.'"

5. 1 Peter 1:13: "So prepare your minds for action and exercise self-control. Put all your hope in the gracious salvation that will come to you when Jesus Christ is revealed to the world."

6. Philippians 4:8: "Fix your thoughts on what is true, and honorable, and right, and pure, and lovely, and admirable. Think about things that are excellent and worthy of praise."

7. Psalm 94:19: "When anxiety was great within me, your consolation brought me joy."

8. Psalm 139:23-24: "Search me, O God, and know my heart; test me and know my anxious thoughts. Point out anything in me that offends you, and lead me along the path of everlasting life."

9. Colossians 3:2: "Think about the things of heaven, not the things of earth."

10. Jeremiah 29:11: "'For I know the plans I have for you,' declares the Lord, 'plans to prosper you and not to harm you, plans to give you hope and a future.'"

11. Hebrews 12:1-2: "…let us run with endurance the race God has set before us. We do this by keeping our eyes on Jesus, the champion who initiates and perfects our faith…"

12. Luke 12:25: "Who of you by worrying can add a single hour to your life?"

13. Psalm 119:76: "May your unfailing love be my comfort, according to your promise to your servant."

11 OVERTHINKING QUOTES TO REMEMBER

1. "I get anxious about everything. I just can't stop thinking about things all the time. And here's the really destructive part—it's always retrospective. I waste time thinking of what I should have said or done."—Hugh Laurie

2. "Take time to deliberate, but when the time for action has arrived, stop thinking and go in."—Napoleon Bonaparte

3. "Thinking too much leads to paralysis by analysis. It's important to think things through, but many use thinking as a means of avoiding action."—Robert Herjavek

4. "Worrying is like paying a debt you don't owe."—Mark Twain

5. "Don't brood. Get on with living and loving. You don't have forever."—Leo Buscaglia

6. "Spend 80% of your time focusing on the opportunities of tomorrow rather than the problems of yesterday."—Brian Tracy

7. "Don't get too deep, it leads to overthinking, and overthinking leads to problems that doesn't even exist in the first place."—Jayson Engay

8. "I think and think and think, I've thought myself out of happiness one million times, but never once into it."—Jonathan Safran Foer

9. "You don't have to see the whole staircase, just take the first step."—Martin Luther King, Jr.

10. "The sharpest minds often ruin their lives by overthinking the next step, while the dull win the race with eyes closed."—Bethany Brookbank

11. "If you treat every situation as a life and death matter, you'll die a lot of times."—Dean Smith

References

Tomuletiu, E., Oroian, M., Girbovan, O., Girbovan, C., Buicu, G., & Gyorgy, M. (2014). The impact of communication in the harmonization of couple relationships. *Procedia - Social and Behavioral Sciences, 116*, 5041–5045. doi:10.1016/j.sbspro.2014.01.1070

Siegmann, E., Müller, H., Luecke, C., Philipsen, A., Kornhuber, J., & Grömer, T. (2018). Association of depression and anxiety disorders with autoimmune thyroiditis: A systematic review and meta-analysis. *JAMA Psychiatry, 75*(6), 577–584. doi:10.1001/jamapsychiatry.2018.0190

Laursen, B., & Hafen, C. (2010). Future directions in the study of close relationships: Conflict is bad (except when it's not). *Social Development, 19*(4), 858–872. doi:10.1111/j.1467-9507.2009.00546.x

Lavner, J., Karney, B., & Bradbury, T. (2016). Does couples' communication predict marital satisfaction, or does marital satisfaction predict communication? *Journal of Marriage and Family, 78*(3), 680–694. doi:10.1111/jomf.12301

Michl, L., McLaughlin, K., Shepherd, K., & Nolen-Hoeksema, S. (2013).

Rumination as a mechanism linking stressful life events to symptoms of depression and anxiety: Longitudinal evidence in early adolescents and adults. *Journal of Abnormal Psychology, 122*(2), 339–352. doi:10.1037/a0031994

Moland, M. (2011). *Conflict and satisfaction in romantic relationships* (thesis). Fort Hays State University. Retrieved from https://scholars.fhsu.edu/theses/154.

Nguyen, D., Wright, E., Dedding, C., Pham, T., & Bunders, J. (2019). Low self-esteem and its association with anxiety, depression, and suicidal ideation in Vietnamese secondary school students: A cross-sectional study. *Frontiers in Psychiatry, 10*. doi:10.3389/fpsyt.2019.00698

Rogers, S., Howieson, J., & Neame, C. (2018). I understand you feel that way, but I feel this way: The benefits of I-language and communicating perspective during conflict. *PeerJ, 6*. doi:10.7717/peerj.4831.

Tsatsoulis, A., & Fountoulakis, S. (2006). The protective role of exercise on stress system dysregulation and comorbidities. *Annals of the New York Academy of Sciences, 1083*, 196–213. doi:10.1196/annals.1367.020

Tseng, J., & Poppenk, J. (2020). Brain meta-state transitions demarcate thoughts across task contexts exposing the mental noise of trait neuroticism. *Nature Communications, 11*, 3480. doi:10.1038/s41467-020-17255-9

U.S. Department of Health and Human Services. (2020). *Obsessive-compulsive disorder: When unwanted thoughts or repetitive behaviors take over*. National Institute of Mental Health. Retrieved from https://www.nimh.nih.gov/health/publications/obsessive-compulsive-disorder-when-unwanted-thoughts-take-over

Watkins, E., & Roberts, H. (2020). Reflecting on rumination: Consequences, causes, mechanisms and treatment of rumination. *Behaviour Research and Therapy, 127*, 103573. doi:10.1016/j.brat.2020.103573

University of Southern California. (2015). Words can deceive, but tone of voice cannot: Voice tone analyses of therapy sessions accurately predict whether relationships will improve. *ScienceDaily*. Retrieved from www.sciencedaily.com/releases/2015/11/151123202344.htm

www.ingramcontent.com/pod-product-compliance
Lightning Source LLC
Chambersburg PA
CBHW070742060526
44119CB00071B/126